I Am Now

Kristie Dean

First published by Busybird Publishing 2017
Copyright © 2017 Kristie Dean

ISBN
Print: 978-1-925585-95-7
Ebook: 978-1-925585-77-3

Kristie Dean has asserted her right under the Copyright, Designs and Patents Act 1988 to be identified as the author of this work. The information in this book is based on the author's experiences and opinions. The publisher specifically disclaims responsibility for any adverse consequences, which may result from use of the information contained herein. Permission to use information has been sought by the author. Any breaches will be rectified in further editions of the book.

All rights reserved. No part of this publication may be reproduced, stored in or introduced into a retrieval system, or transmitted in any form, or by any means (electronic, mechanical, photocopying, recording or otherwise) without the prior written permission of the author. Any person who does any unauthorised act in relation to this publication may be liable to criminal prosecution and civil claims for damages. Enquiries should be made through the publisher.

Cover image: Robert Koenig Luck
Chapter images: Rahel Raeber
Cover design: Busybird Publishing
Layout and typesetting: Busybird Publishing
Editor: Laura McCluskey

Busybird Publishing
2/118 Para Road
Montmorency, Victoria
Australia 3094
www.busybird.com.au

Contents

Introduction	i
My Soul Arrives	1
Shattered	13
The Confession / Dear Brother	21
Just a Little Nipper	27
Healing Hands	35
Listen, Act, and Survive	43
Sisterly Love	53
Moving and Thriving	57
Releasing and Letting Go	65
Insight Visions	77
The CML Bomb	81
The Fight of My Life	93
International Mum	103
Words from My International Family	113
New York, Amazon Jungle	119
Flashes of Life	129
Changing the Scales	143
I Am Now	151
Your one word?	163
Acknowledgements	165
About the Author	169
Kristie as a Speaker	173
I Was Then – Exploring Past Lives	175
The Book of Inspirations for Women by Women	177
Where is Kristie NOW - Update 2023	179
Carolyn Trethewey-Wellness Advocate	183
Busybird Publishing	185
Ultimate 48 Hour Author	187

Testimonials

'Ladies and gentlemen, I present to you the future of our great country, and an inspiration for people all around the world. **Bubbling under the surface**, intelligence overwhelming, this woman with wild wings is a delight and surprise from within.

>K is for kid, the child within.
>R is for rational, the way you think.
>I is for ignite, the fire in you!
>S is for sweet, your pleasing way.
>T is for touching, the way you show.
>I is for impress, for impress you will.
>E is for expressive, not one to hold within.
>
>D is for dashing, the romantic you!
>E is for enjoy, your life can be fun!
>A is for agreeable, the best side of you!
>N is for noble, your regal bearing.'

>Darren Baverstock,
>*Meditation teacher, Sydney, Australia*

'Our friendship has become a sisterhood over the last 30 years. It has been a journey full of laughs, sorrow, frustration, mentoring, match-making, and a bond that will be forever! Kristie's resilience has made her the woman she is today. The circumstances that she has had to overcome has not stopped her from fulfilling her dreams and drive to live for today. Her passion, **determination** and love for life has been an inspiration to many, including me.'

>Heidi Allison,
>*Perth, Western Australia*

'Kristie is an inspiration, she has a gift for it and I know she will inspire you within these pages. The day we first met, Kristie shared with me her goal to write a book about her life. I remember there was such strength and determination behind those words. I had no doubt Kristie would bring her dream to life.

Synchronicity is a theme through both of our lives and it was exciting to be part of the universe's plan to guide Kristie to her publisher. The level of enthusiasm and dedication Kristie has put into crafting the chapters of her book is nothing short of amazing!

Most recently, when Kristie became unwell prior to her book retreat (an integral part of the process) it was tough to see her struggle. Once again, Kristie's strength shone through. Kristie focused her resolve on overcoming all obstacles and in the process healed herself deeply. All by being true to who she is and the message she has to share from her heart to yours.

I know you will love this book! Kristie – I am blessed to have you as a treasured friend. Can't wait to witness where your book journey takes you next!'

        Carolyn Trethewey,

        Director of Pause – people.animals.wellness, Perth, Western Australia

'Kristie is my partner's sister. I have known her for 22 years, although I didn't really get to know her well until she moved to Perth 18 years ago. When I first met Kristie I thought, wow, she is gorgeous. It was 1994, and she was skinny with big boobs, blonde hair, and a great complexion. We were up North in the Pilbara when Kristie was diagnosed with leukaemia and were unable to offer anything more than our thoughts and best wishes as she went through that awful time in her life.

I was amazed by her strength and perseverance to just keep moving forward even when faced with the misfortune of childhood trauma, diagnoses and management of leukaemia, and loss of her body shape due to all the medication and steroids she was on.

What I saw was this dynamic person caring for overseas students. She created a home away from home for them. She kept the house clean and tidy. You could have eaten your dinner off any surface in the house. She was cooking wonderful, healthy meals each evening for the students. They would sit down to dinner together and talk about their day. Kristie would place an **inspirational** card down at each person's place at the table so they could reflect on it before dinner. Over the years there has often been foreign students spending Christmas with our extended family or joining us on a trip somewhere. It has been enriching. Kristie also had a wonderful doggie companion called Sam. He had a lovely nature and was very special. Unfortunately, he has passed away.

When Kristie was feeling good she would pour everything she had into caring for the students. Her students still love and respect her and keep in touch. Some of them have been back to Perth to visit. She was definitely a mother to all of them at one time or another.

Throughout Kristie's life she has had many up and downs. Some people might have fallen into a heap and not been able to pull themselves up, out of it. Kristie always has such positive energy and vitality and those around her can't help but be swept up in it. Her ability to keep looking forward and not dwell on the past is her strength.'

  Debbie Robinson,
  Perth, Australia

'Kristie came into my life back in 2010 when I was down and out, and she welcomed me with open arms. She has been able to guide me through **challenging times** to this day. Her energy and peace within can change any negative thoughts you have towards something in life. This is a true skillset that Kristie holds naturally, and is greatly appreciated by me and I'm sure a lot more. Thanks, Kristie.'

Dane Lyons,
Owner/Director Lyons Trading Pty. Ltd.,
Australia

'It was in 2012 (end of the year) and I really needed a break after a troubled year. I booked a flight to Australia without accommodation, and afterwards I looked around on the internet for a room. I wrote to several people, but got no answer. After 24 hours, I got an answer from Kristie.

When I arrived, Kristie came out and gave me a big hug. The ice was broken and this was the beginning of a special connection. We had a great time together and talked for days and nights. Most of the time we talked about spirituality and unconditional love. It was like we'd known each other for the lifetime.

She invited me to celebrate Christmas with her family, and I have now spent many Christmases with Kristie's family since then, whom I now call my "Australian Family".

I now have a beautiful soulmate on my side. She is an absolutely warm, optimistic, and **open-minded** person. I will not lose her in my life. She shared with me a lot of her stories from her life and I am amazed that she still can keep smiling. She has a strong personality and I just love her.'

Rahel Raeber,
Switzerland

Dedication

Jill McNair (nee Horne), I dedicate this book to you. Thank you for showing me a way of life when I was a young teenager and teaching me how to heal my body. I know that we've lived in other lives before this one together. Your unconditional love and healing support paved the way for me in my teenage years, opening life's possibilities and my path that was meant to be. We lost contact for 25 years but we found each other again. It was all meant to be, and at the right time.

You have helped me again, supporting me as I wrote this book with your **powerful guidance** and your spiritual healing. I wouldn't have done it without you and I'm glad that you have been by my side. Thank you, Jill, and thank you also from all the thousands of people who you have helped heal around the world. You are truly a powerful healing energy spirit. I have been nothing but blessed to have had you intermittently in my life.

That one special, almost unexplainable day you helped me in early April of 2017, just before the final stages of my book were completed, allowed me to fully release the supressed energy of my childhood. It was nothing but profound, extraordinary, powerful **beyond words**, and has changed my path forever ...

This powerful healing was meant to be and could have only been done by you, my spiritual Mother.

Introduction

*'Your own **self-realization** is the greatest service you can render the world.'*

– Ramana Maharshi

We all have a story inside of us. I've decided to share mine with you.

I've had a piping hot desire inside of me over the last few years to tell my story. I felt that it was just something that I absolutely had to do. It took months and a lot of **deep thought** and time with myself to work out how this was going to happen – how I was going to write it, what I wanted to deliver, and how I wanted to tell my story.

For a start, I'm quite dyslexic, so I knew that it was not going to be easy for me to sit down and just write. I knew it would challenge me, but that I would learn to overcome it as I would never let being dyslexic hold me back in any way. At first I tried to find a program that would transcribe my words into text. I knew that telling my story needed to come from my heart and flow straight out of me, like I'm having a conversation with you.

Towards the end of 2016 I'd just got back from a trip over in Queensland, and writing my book was still on my mind. I'd been home one week and my whole mind was consumed with it. I could feel the passion inside me. I just had to listen to myself and trust what my mind and heart was trying to tell me. I got a phone call from my girlfriend Carolyn asking if I wanted to join her in a seminar about writing a book. She already had her ticket and said they offered her the opportunity to take a friend. I remember that I felt like dropping on my knees in a prayer position. 'Oh my God,' I said to her, 'I've spent the last week in deep thought on how I could write this book! You've just answered my prayers, of course I'm going to be at this course – how do I do it?'

She said she'd send an e-mail asking for me to get the free seat offer, but I was so wowed by the **opportunity**, and so absolutely determined to be at this seminar that I contacted Natasa Denman directly and secured a spot for myself, because there was no way I was going to miss it. I just had this impulse about being there … every part of my body was telling me it was a must.

Everything I learned from Natasa completely resonated with me. She's helped more than 150 other authors produce their books. The biggest thing that appealed to me was the whole procedure – you voice your book and have it transcribed for you. Being dyslexic, this was a big tick, and the way that I could actually see this book coming together. By committing to dates and times and the financial side, I knew that it was going to happen. Within 48 hours of the seminar I was committed, and ready to write my book. I could not have been happier. Just the whole feeling of knowing that I was actually going to make a **lifetime goal** happen was incredible, and then the journey began.

I embrace being a very open soul. My friends will tell you that I've always been an over-sharer. I've loved the entertainment of life unfolding, and the crazy things we would do and say and act and feel. Very amusing to me. Another thing that had been on my mind for quite a few years was being able to follow up on my story of being a cancer survivor. Nearly 16 years ago now, I was diagnosed with leukaemia. I was given a trial drug that saved my life. I was all over the media: *Today Tonight*, *A Current Affair*, Channel 9 News, and the *Sunday Times*, fighting for my life. Since then I have been blessed with a second chance. The drug had put my body into remission and I have stayed that way now for all of these years. Now it is my wish to go public and say thank you. How do you really thank Australia for that? I can't think of a more **powerful** way than to write this book and put it out there.

So, I ask you to be open to me and let my story touch your heart, and maybe even provoke your own emotions. If some of my story reminds you of your own life, let it; feel it, relive it, and heal it if you need to. If anything, enjoy the story, as it's just a story – the one of my heart. And I really wouldn't have it any other way. Embrace it, I say.

You will have noticed, and will find throughout my book, some **bold**, printed words. Words have energy about them, so when you see the bold word, notice it, and read on. I want to surprise you with the reason for this, and it will all make sense when you come to the end of the book. I want you to trust the process and leave the **suspense** until then.

Get a coffee and some snacks, snuggle up, and enjoy my story.

My Soul Arrives

'All bodies emerge from the Soul and return to it.
The visible emerges from the invisible, is **controlled** by it, and returns to it.'

– Lao Russell

It's said before we're even born we get to choose the **journey** that we want to take in this life – the things we need to balance out, what we need to learn, experience, and accomplish. There's a huge number of articles and documents on this subject; our destined journey, how we pick our parents, and when the soul enters the human body. I'm imagining with my personality that I decided right at the last minute who I was going to journey with in this next life.

On 21 November 1971, my soul arrived.

Like the collision of thunder hitting the Earth, my body and soul, *boom*, I was here. Here it goes, the ride of my life! I sensed that I didn't want a plain, boring life. I wanted to experience every kind of feeling that life has to offer. I wanted to feel all the highs and lows coming from every sense in my body, so it was then that I chose my parents. I was tucked up in my mummy's tummy, sensing the excitement building, as I lie in a foetal position.

I felt the energies outside building up for my entrance. What the hell was going to happen next? As I pushed through my mother's opening, my first flight had landed. It was 5:00pm. I was in the town of Bunbury in the south-west of Western Australia, in Saint John of God Hospital. I was second-born through this passage of life, as I discovered much later in life that there had been someone else before me. I was born a healthy little baby girl. They named me Kristie, and I felt the love all around me. What a beautiful and **exhilarating** entrance, full of love and so much excitement.

I continued to grow as the months went along, hitting all the normal milestones a child should. One of my favourite things to do was to rock on my tummy with my arms and legs up in the air. While this is all happening, my mother was growing another life inside her tummy.

I was around 14 months old when panic set in – my temperature was rising, **alarm bells** were going off, my mum was panicking, my nappies had turned green, and my little body was burning up. The rush was on to get me to hospital. My mother was out of breath because she was very pregnant, but she was determined to get those hospital doors open and get me looked at, as she knew something was really not right.

With the doctors and nurse, their full attention was on me. I was feeling very stressed, my body was aching, and I felt like vomiting. After hours of stress and uncertainty, we had a result. I was diagnosed with salmonellosis, an illness caused by bacteria that comes from contaminated food or water, or another person's hand.

How had this happened to me? My intestinal track was on fire and the lining of my stomach felt like it was burning away. My body temperature was out of control and my body was fragile. As time went by I became stable as my body was pumped with antibiotics. I was placed in isolation and had a feeding tube placed down my nose. I was feeling very irritable, and I didn't know what I needed to do for myself. The nurses put mittens on my hands so that I would stop pulling out the nose tube. My father spent days on end just sitting with me while my body got stronger.

I wasn't easy to handle because I wanted someone always with me, but not touching me, so my dad comforted me most of the time – my mother was heavily pregnant, so the only visits I enjoyed with her were through the glass windows from my isolated hospital room. She looked at me with stress and helplessness, and I looked at her and wanted a hug. But it was too dangerous for my brother, who was still growing inside of her.

My grandparents were often at the hospital. They knew one of the doctors so they were constantly getting updates, but they were keeping a lot of information away from my parents to protect them, which was frustrating. Weeks went by, and my fragile little body was healing itself. I was in hospital for around three weeks until we got the word that I was able to go home, but to my grandparent's place because it still wasn't safe for me to have contact with my mother and unborn brother until I was well clear of contamination.

As I was healing away in the safety and comfort – but **isolation** – of my very protective grandparent's house, the health department went into my family home to try to find the cause of the salmonella. They checked the small fish tank that we had at home, the sandpit that I played in often, and the butcher's where the butcher always gave me a piece of yummy baloney on each of my visits, but they could never pinpoint where it had come from.

Suddenly, my mum was rushed to the hospital – my brother Bradley was on his way. As I was still at my grandparents, meeting my new brother took a few more weeks before my mother finally picked me up from my loving grandparents' home. Mum was advised against contact with me, and my grandparents really didn't want me to leave, but she took the chance because she missed me and wanted us all together. So I was finally taken home and I had a new brother.

Life went on, me as a toddler with a little baby brother. I have memories of my three-wheeler bike that I'd peddle down to the back woodshed, helping my dad by filling up the back of my bike with wood for the fireplace we had in the house. We had a guinea pig who would always be in his cage, except for when our pet cockatiel would undo the latch and let my guinea pig out, and the search would be on. I remember having pet ducks to play with, and being fascinated by them. I would pick their furry little bodies up and make them run across the little pond my dad had made them, tiring them out.

You would always find me not far away from my empty pillow case that I had the habit of carrying around and rubbing the corners for comfort, alongside my favourite thumb in my mouth. One afternoon, I went missing. I can remember my parents calling out for me, but I didn't want to tell them where I was, as I'd climbed my way up onto the carport and was hanging off the top of the roof. My parents couldn't believe it one day when they looked up and saw me up there, not making a word. I really don't remember how they got me down, but I know that if I had have slipped I may not be here today …

When I was around four years old, my parents decided that it was time for a new location and **venture** – time for my parents to get some space away from my grandparents, to feel more grown up, without their meddling. So, we packed up most of the family belongings in the car and headed north to Carnarvon, Western Australia. We moved into a caravan park in the town, which was located about 900km north of Perth. This was exciting for me as a child, because it was my first experience living in a caravan park, and there were lots of other children to play with and lots of things to explore.

I experienced kindergarten, then my first year of primary school. I loved primary school. I remember sitting in class one day with my legs and arms crossed and my back straight to get attention from my teacher; I enjoyed being the teacher's pet. I remember one day in class I accidentally wet my pants. I felt so humiliated. The teacher started scrambling through the lost property box and found me a pair of old tee-ball pants to put on, and that was like putting on a pair of clown pants. Gee, I was really thankful to have some dry pants, but a big pair of old tee-ball pants? How embarrassing! This wasn't the attention I was craving.

Life in the caravan park was lots of fun. I can remember spending hours upon hours in the swimming pool, practising my diving. I played with all the other kids and we had adventures, and created imaginary games. There was a lot more freedom in those days, but there was also **confusion**, as the police came to visit us a few times. They removed everything we owned from inside our caravan and placed them out in the street for everyone to see, as they were looking for drugs. I believe we had to move caravan parks a few times in Carnarvon, because this was a recurring thing.

On Mother's Day 1977, I remember waking up feeling very excited because I had a gift for my mum that I'd made at school. I'd been counting the days until I could give it to her, but to my surprise, my mum wasn't home that morning. I remember feeling quite unsure and shocked – where was Mum? I asked my grandparents who were staying with us as it was nearly time for my next brother to be born, and they'd come to lend a hand. Well, the time had come, and a hand was needed – my mum had been taken to hospital and was giving birth to my brother, Jay. How exciting and confusing at the same time; I just wanted to give her the gift I had made, but my brother was arriving. At six years old, having a little brother to play with was just as good as receiving a real little doll. Jay was born healthy and well without any complications, popping out quickly into the world.

Jay was only six weeks old when we were on the move again. The brand new caravan Mum and Dad had purchased was all packed up and we were headed further north again, up the Western Australian coastline, arriving in a town called Roebourne, about 1563km north of Perth, or 202km south of Port Hedland. Roebourne was former gold rush town in the 19th century and was once the largest settlement between Darwin and Perth. Our new home was in another caravan park. I remember the park to be very busy, full of new arrivals because the word was out that there was a lot of work in the Pilbara mining industry, and the new settlement town of Wickham was settling its foundations only 13km away. The Pilbara, the red dirt country, was attracting lots of young families who were all looking for new money and new starts.

This caravan park was even bigger than the one in Carnarvon, with a lot more people and excitement around. I still needed to finish off my first year of school, so I attended Roebourne Primary School. The children going to this school were mostly Indigenous, so I was only one of a few white Australian girls who went there. This was fun, but also very different. I have **memories** of running around in the schoolyard and, in the undercover areas, playing hopscotch, and with my hula hoop. I was such a little blondie, very fair skin, white hair, blue eyes, and was a bit of a tomboy, and I loved putting my hair in pigtails.

I can remember playing games like Indians and Itchy Bums (but I can't really remember how that went). I was introduced to the local Aboriginal language, and this was awesome fun as we could play around with a lot of new words. I remember knowing the word 'jungerna' that meant 'emu'. I also knew the word 'munda' that was 'rock'. Sometimes when you lied, you could say that you were 'thutthey'. We'd often giggle and laugh, teasing each other. We would try to scare each other with the 'munbreen ngarda' (Aboriginal spirit man). We would say it was behind you, chasing you, and it was going to get you! I often remember running around with no shoes on, and this being quite a normal thing.

I remember sitting at my dining table, doing my reading homework after school. This is when I realised for the first time that there was something wrong with my reading ability. I'd try really hard and get frustrated. I wanted to be able to please my teachers, but I struggled. Words were just not my thing. I remember having arguments with my mum a lot. I couldn't understand why this was so difficult, as in those days no one could explain to me how the dyslexic mind worked.

One day after school I was heading up to catch the bus back to the caravan park, which we did daily. I would have been about seven years old, and I had my yellow suitcase with me. We were messing around as kids do, playing games while **waiting** for the bus. One of the girls took my suitcase and was filling it with red dirt and a horseshoe that she must have picked up somewhere. This made me super furious, so my automatic instinct was to punch her in the nose. With blood running out of her nose, I started to panic because I knew that when the bus driver pulled up and saw what was going on, I was going to be in big trouble. Without thinking it through, I picked up my suitcase and decided to walk home.

I had a pretty good idea of the way there – I remember crossing a few roads and walking down through the dry riverbank, which I had to then cross and walk into the bush. I followed some paths and hoped to goodness that I would arrive somewhere near the caravan park. I'm guessing this would have taken me a good 30-45 minutes to get there, and luckily for me I did. I ended up on a back track in the caravan park, but by then word had gotten out that I wasn't on the bus, so my father was standing there waiting for me. I was terrified because I could hear him yelling and screaming at me before I even got close to him. He kicked my butt so high I can remember flying in the air. Aw, man, what pain that was.

I have so many **amazing** experiences of living in the Roebourne caravan park; there were so many places to go, and I could build cubby houses and meet with my friends, and often be hanging around in the toilet blocks doing something. Our parents were quite comfortable just letting us go off and play because it was like living with one big family, and in those days you never really had much to worry about. I have memories of getting together with other kids and playing in different caravan annexes, pegging up sheets and making portend hospitals to play doctors and nurses. We were always using our creative imaginations to play with anything fun we could find.

I was playing outside our caravan with my brothers one day. Jay was about two years old at the time, and we were playing with a set of children's tables and chairs. We were stacking them up on top of each other, making a tower. When I wasn't looking, I heard a crash. Jay had climbed up on the tower and it had collapsed. My father came running. Jay looked lifeless; he'd stopped **breathing**. My father picked him up and was panicking, as you can imagine. He started yelling at me, 'Kristie, you've killed your brother!'

I didn't understand what was going on, other than the fact that my brother was going blue and wasn't breathing. A lady came running. Her name was Doreen, and she was a nurse. My father was begging for help, so Doreen took Jay, and he started breathing. Oh, thank goodness for that. Everyone was in shock. It was like time had stood still. It was a scene you didn't want to be involved in, and witness. Afterwards, my father was still angry and reminded me that I almost killed my brother. This moment will never leave me; it **shocked** me to the core.

Moving forward, I remember my little brother Jay being about three years old, and we moved 10km away to the town of Wickham, a little mining town. The town had just become open to public housing, and a new home was waiting for us. It was on a street called Nelly Way. The family was all so excited – a new house, and so much bigger than the caravan! We had our own backyard and front yard! Houses were being constructed everywhere, and streets were popping up all over the town. It was really cool because it felt like most of the people who'd lived in the caravan park were moving into Wickham, too, so I had still had friends everywhere. I moved to Wickham Primary School. Most of the kids from the school in Roebourne were already going to the Wickham school way before I was. There were only a select few of us who were going to the Roebourne school first, so it was a change.

The population of Wickham has only ever really hovered around the 2000 mark. Wickham was a really exciting place to grow up in, and everyone I know has always looked back at it with fond memories. It was a huge sporting **community**, and I started playing tee-ball, a really popular game. It's a bit like baseball, but we hit a ball off a stick called the tee. My team wore blue, and we were called the Dolphins. This little town was full of different sports to play as a kid, and had a huge supportive community – it was a very special place to grow up.

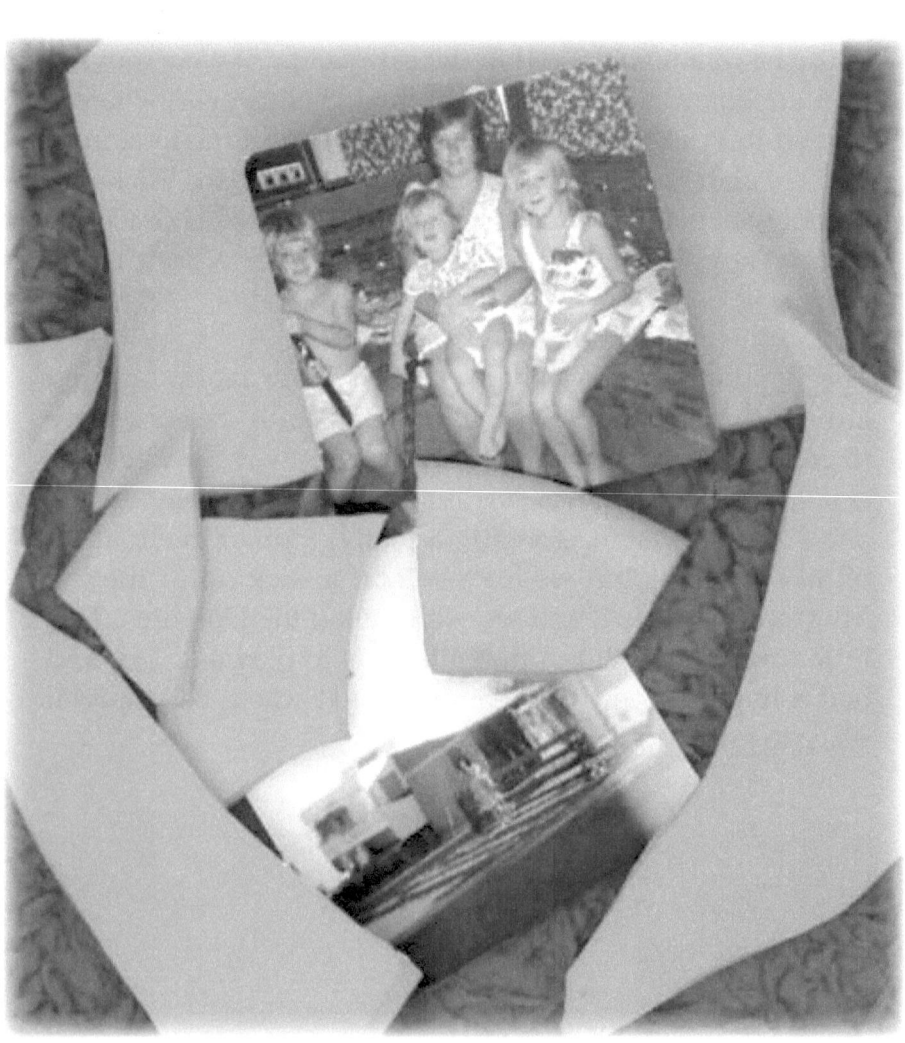

Shattered

'For all our insight, obstinate habits do not disappear until replaced by other habits ... No amount of **confession** and no amount of explaining can make the crooked plant grow straight; it must be trained upon the trellis by the gardener's art ...'

– Carl Jung

It was normal for me to hear a lot of bad language in my house, coming from my father. A lot of the time he was very abusive and argumentative. He was also quite a **perfectionist**, so if something wasn't performed the way he wanted it done, an argument would start and his mouth would be in full force. It was pretty constant, because none of us could do anything right. This definitely caused a very uneasy feeling in the air.

It always felt like we had a lot of visitors hanging around our house. My father had built a big pergola in the backyard of our new home, and was always making pathways or planting and building something, almost obsessively. There was talk about drugs, and the smell of marijuana was common; it would be sitting in a bag somewhere on the table, or my dad would be smoking it. I remember conversations about how to grow and sell marijuana … nothing was ever hidden.

My father was abusive to my mother, and often physically abusive with all of us. My brother Bradley, in particular, was an easy target because he had a placid personality, and my father's anger would be taken out on him more than me. If you even sat on the lounge chair the wrong way, you were told to get out and pushed around. The simple things in life often had a twist, of being the wrong way to my father. As a child, I remember always feeling on edge and nervous, never really knowing what was going to happen next. I never had that feeling of safety and security in my own home, always **wondering** if I was going to get thrown around, or hear and watch my mother and brother being abused. His emotions would go up and down – a lot of anger, to snippets of love where my father was gentle and would do anything for me.

This was confusing in our little minds, because we just didn't know what we were going to get. It was very exhausting.

You never knew when you were sitting down for a family dinner (always a good meat and vegetables) what was going to come out of my dad's mouth. You never knew whether the dinner plate was going to go flying across the room, and that happened many times over the years. If you didn't eat your vegetables, or something else happened, he would get fired up really quickly. In a second your dinner could be thrown through the air, or you were sent to your room, pushed about, or just simply verbally abused. My father would sometimes pick me up by the throat and push me against the wall if I'd done something wrong in his eyes. He often kept this behaviour to a minimum when other people from outside the family were around, however, it really didn't stop him – when he was going to fire off, he would just do it. This often made our visitors quite uncomfortable because it would stop everyone in their tracks, and no one really knew how to react or what to do. It wasn't **unusual** for me to find bruises on my arms or legs from being pushed around a lot.

I remember one night my father was with my mother in the bedroom and he was abusing, and **threatening** her. I could hear her screaming and crying. My brother and I were terrified. I think Jay was in bed, as I only remember Bradley being with me out the back in the garden. We were just hugging each other under a small tree, so frightened. We couldn't go in the house, there was so much abuse and anger going on. We were just bawling our eyes out, terrified. It was horrible.

When my grandparents came to stay, which they often did, they would drive their caravan up from Bunbury. It always felt like they were fearful of my father, too, because of his erratic behaviour and his verbal abuse. It was very difficult for my grandparents to see this, but when they'd tell him they didn't like the way he was behaving it would just make him crazier, so everyone would try to keep a lid on it. For me this was normal, so I didn't know that other families weren't the same. But I would question everything and always get into trouble, because I was always wanting to please and be a good girl.

I would often have **conversations** with my father telling him that I didn't understand why he was like this, and why was he hitting me when I was trying to do my best. Most of these deeper conversations where you could actually talk to my father happened when he was sitting outside smoking pot, as this calmed his system down. It was like living with two personalities; the father on pot, a crazy bloke off it. When he did smoke he was softer, and there was a more relaxed environment. You didn't know what you were going to get. I was always very nervous as a child.

It was common for my father to bring people home from the pub. We often had other people staying with us for days on end with their vans on our property. One lady who stayed with us introduced me to massage therapy. She enjoyed showing me how to do a foot massage routine. I was intrigued by this; it was my first experience being able to use my hands in a healing way. It really resonated with me. She had also introduced me to stories about God and some teachings about *The Bible*, which I'd never heard much of before because my family wasn't religious. She even took me to the local church one day, and I remember really enjoying this and having those deeper conversations with her about life, even though I was only about eight years old. We'd formed quite a strong bond just within a few weeks, and my massage skills and connections were getting stronger. I remember feeling very in tune with these massages, even at my young age. I guess it was probably a connection to feeling more relaxed and at ease, because my family life was so crazy and erratic, so this was a form of healing for me.

When I'd just turned nine years old, a little nipper, my spirit was shattered. It was a Sunday. It had been a **relaxing afternoon**, and we'd had visitors around. I think that they were still around in the lounge, or outside at the pool table area. Everyone was doing their own thing. I was asked to give a massage, and I agreed and was excited by this, as I had been learning a lot of new skills and I was very good at it. I was guided into my parents' bedroom. He was wearing a sarong, as he usually did. I started massaging his feet and up his legs, and this continued for a while until I felt his hand guiding mine closer to his pelvic area. He then moved my little hands over his penis.

I remember the stress and the pressure building in my head. I didn't really understand, it didn't seem right, but I'd trusted this person, and also feared him. He continued guiding my hands back and forward over his penis and around his balls. I almost went into shock. I remember feeling like I was doing it – I didn't want to be doing it, but I didn't stop it from happening. I remember feeling really tight in my stomach as he then placed his fingers inside of my vagina. I was almost too scared to breathe. I wanted time to stop, as if that was going to make me feel like this wasn't happening and it would all go away. His fingers were moving in and out of me and it was hurting deeply and very violently. I was too scared to make a noise, so I was holding it all in. It was almost like I was **meditating** to try to turn off the pain. I remember feeling the energy in my body, like nothing I'd felt before. It was intense disbelief. After this went on for some time and the pressure to not yell out was very intense, he took his hands off me, rolled over, and fell asleep.

The details of this abuse have always been super clear to me, as though it is etched in my soul. I was freaking out inside. It was hard to explain the intensity. I didn't want to move an inch. I was waiting for him to fall asleep so I could escape the room. After what seemed like an hour, my mind came around and said, 'Right, get the hell out of here'. I jumped out of his bed and went into my own bedroom and closed the door. I needed **solitude**, and I needed to feel safe. I did not understand what had happened. My brain was processing it. I was shattered, I was broken. I felt different; my stomach was in knots, and the whole reality of my life had suddenly just changed. My soul had been violated. He broke it. My sense and **awareness** of life had suddenly changed. I was highly alert of my surroundings – stuck in a fight or flight response.

The Confession / Dear Brother

'To my brother, forgive me for my pain.
Forgive me for your pain.
For you are my brother, always.
I love you.'
– Kristie Dean

I guess when you write a book it's probably a good idea to confess something, and this one always made me feel awkward and uncomfortable. At the same time it was part of my life, and we've grown up now. Looking back at it, it's good for me to get this one off my chest. So, let me tell you ...

We had a family car growing up, a cute, old-fashioned Holden FB, and it was my father's pride and joy. It was a two-toned kind of green station wagon, and we had it for years. I was around ten years old – a couple of months before the incident – when this car went for a brand-new paint job, and it came back looking fabulous. To **be honest**, I think my first love of old-style cars came from us having this car, as it was a part of our family.

On the weekends my dad would take the three of us kids outside and we'd be given a rag each while my dad was in charge of the can of Mr Sheen. We Mr Sheened this car completely, every inch of it as my father ran around, until this beautiful green-toned car was just shining. It seems quite peculiar, because I don't think I've heard of anyone Mr Sheen-ing their car before, but that's how proud my father was of it.

I mentioned earlier that I met this lady who was teaching me massage, and that she would often take me down to the local church in this short period of time in my life when she introduced me to God. On one of these trips she purchased a little cross on a necklace for me, and I was very proud of it; it was the first cross I'd ever had. It was only a few months after our car had been painted when the incident occurred. I really can't remember what the mood was, or why I did it, but I got the cross – which had really sharp edges – and I etched my brother's initials into the car. It was small, but really **noticeable.** And it was such a horrible thing to do, because I did it to get him into trouble, I'm guessing. I completely denied that it was me and, of course, my brother denied it, too. No one saw me do it, and the fact that it was done with a little cross from the church felt like such a big sin.

In this book, I officially confess. I am so sorry to my brother, because I love him to bits and he is a very important person in my life. But Brother, I confess. I love you and I am so, so, so sorry. I hope that God will forgive me for this, but I really, truly felt so bad that I knew I had to confess completely.

I AM SORRY, BROTHER!

Just a Little Nipper

'Every tree and plant in the meadow seemed to be **dancing,** those which average eyes would see as fixed and still.'

– Rumi

As I continued growing as a little girl, my mind was never far from that tragic sexual violation. The fear, the unease it caused … the core of me was changed. My energy as a little human had changed. The tension in my body was always there. I could feel my immune system struggling. I would lay in my bedroom a lot and think about life, about the space around me, and wonder how I was to fit into this world. I know it was a feeling of uncertainty. I was carrying the stress of that violation in my body, every moment of every day. It was taking my energy. I was feeling tired a lot. Life needed to go on, but it was never made easy with the fact that that sexual violator was my own father.

Habits were formed where I would have to sleep with my door closed, even though I would not access the air conditioning coming from the back of the house in the heat. My father had stumbled in my room a few times in the weeks and months after that incident. I woke up in the middle of the night to find him stumbling over me, pretending to pull up the sheets. I never really understood what was going on, other than that I didn't feel comfortable. I demanded he leave the room. I'm not sure if he was under the **influence** of drugs or alcohol, but I know it wasn't right. He'd done it once and I bet he thought he could do it again. I know that I also formed the habit of feeling more comfortable in pyjama pants. I was never a nightie girl – that made me feel uncomfortable. I think the pyjama pants gave me the security, and I still wear them now.

With my school life, I continued to struggle with my spelling and reading, so reading became something that I tried to avoid. My school report cards always highlighted the same things: 'Kristie's **enthusiasm** is infectious, but she is easily distracted. She could apply herself more'. I was always in the 'special reading and spelling' group. Sport was my passion, the one area in which I would lead the way, a result of growing up in a small mining town that was all about sports. I spent years practising taekwondo, and I really loved it. I had a nickname at one stage; they would call me 'Wickham's Secret Weapon'. I loved playing netball and being involved in the swimming club. I did aerobics 2-3 times a week.

The town oval was the meeting place for us young kids growing up in Wickham; we would meet day and night. I met my first boyfriend at the age of 11. We had dated for almost a year before I lost my virginity. That was just before I had my first period. Oh, my God – so young, but I remember feeling so old at the time. I look back at that little girl; she was scared and very unsure of how to fit into the world, always on edge from her father's unpredictability. And she just wanted to feel loved and safe.

I know now that that first boyfriend helped me fill that gap, and we were on and off until I was 21. We had first lived together when I was 17 years old. My first pregnancy was at the age of 18, which prompted a trip to Perth for an abortion. It was scary and very emotional. I remember coming out of sedation from the operation too early and screaming in pain, as I could feel the gush of stuff being pulled out of me. A horrifying memory, one that I wish I never had. The second time I fell pregnant I was only 19. I was still living with my boyfriend, and decided I would have the baby. I had been working then for years at the local day-care centre, and loved children. I was always **fascinated** with their minds and I loved finding new positive ways to communicate with them.

At three months into the pregnancy I miscarried, during one of the Pilbara cyclones. I remember laying on the couch having strong abdominal pain and thinking that it was not right. I wasn't getting any bleeding with the pain, so I was advised to get to hospital. There were no doctors around because of the cyclone alert, so I had to get myself to the next town an hour away. I remember lying on that hospital bed as the doctor did an ultrasound, putting that cold gel on my tummy and moving it around to see if they could hear a heartbeat. The seconds seemed to go so slow, but no, there was no heartbeat. It was a very surreal feeling – one minute I had a baby growing inside me, and then there was nothing, no heartbeat. It was so sad. The nurses soon prepared me to have a curette and clean out the remains of the pregnancy. The whole experience was traumatising.

I can remember even weeks and months after I would have moments where I would look at little children and think, 'That could have been my child'. It was difficult because I imagined what that baby was going to look like and how things were going to be, but my dream was shattered. Miscarrying is a real loss. Your body goes through a real **mourning**. It's nothing you can fast track, it just takes time.

Only days away from turning 21, I found out that I was pregnant for the third time. This was a huge shock, because I had separated from my boyfriend and moved back home to Mum and Dad. I'd already decided in my head that having a child with this boyfriend wasn't going to be. I knew at that age that my future was no longer going to be with this boyfriend, almost the only man that I'd loved. We had lived together for years and it was just a life that I didn't want to lead anymore. The shock of being pregnant again was one of those, 'What the hell?' moments. I spent days in deep thought, imagining what my life would be if Option 1 or Option 2 was taken. Two days before my huge 21st birthday party, my mum drove me to the hospital in Port Hedland, about a two and a half hours away in 40 degree heat. It all happened in a day. I got to the hospital, had the abortion, and was out in a few hours and on our way back to Wickham.

I wanted more for my life; I no longer liked the idea of growing up in a small mining town. I wanted to go and **conquer the world**. I had a new attitude and confidence.

Kristie,

You must be so proud of what you have achieved in life,

as are all of us who know and love you.

You have worked so hard and overcome so many obstacles.

I am so proud of you,

You followed your heart in writing this book.

I love the woman you have become.

I love you,

Mum

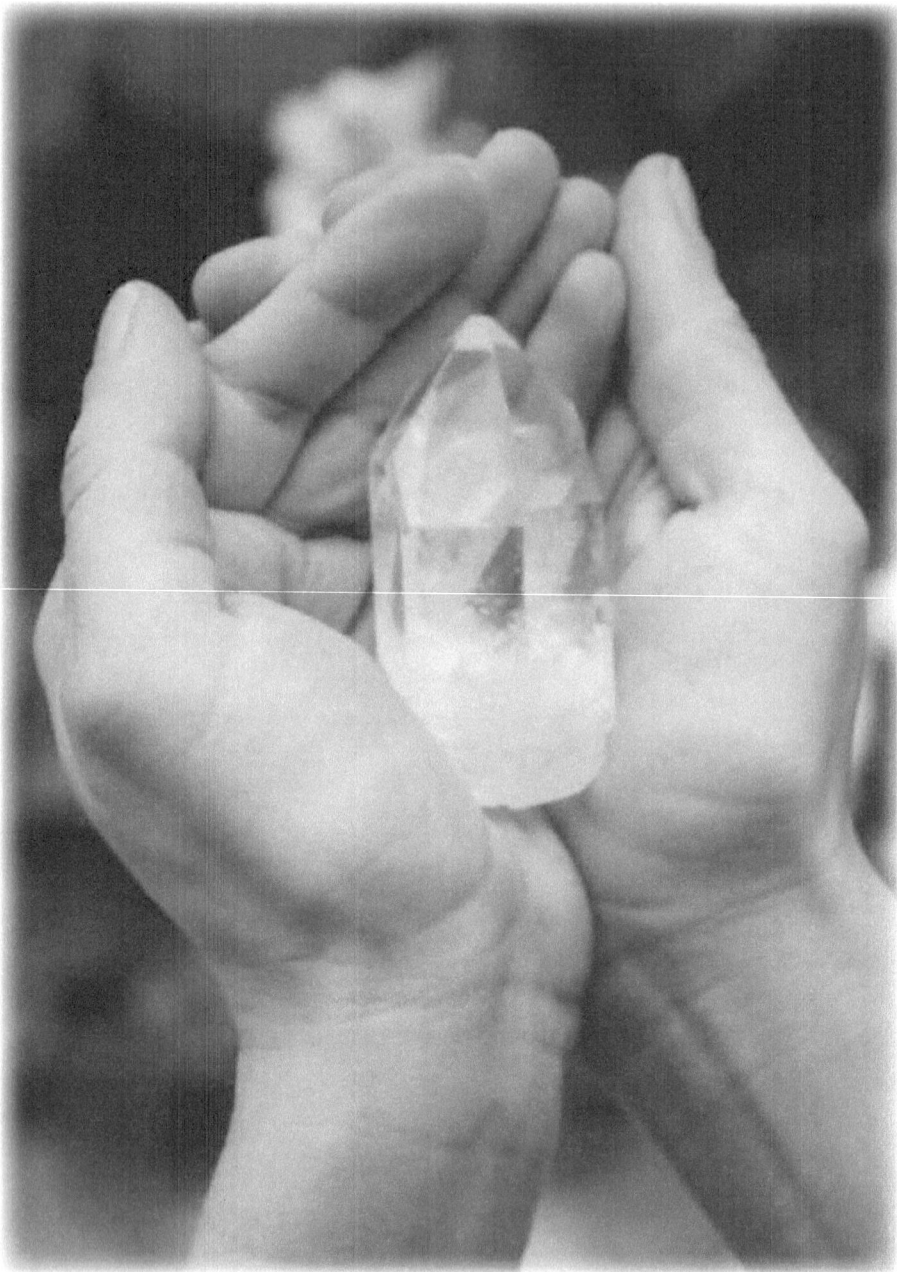

Healing Hands

'**Healing** doesn't come from your body, it is from your Soul.'

– Kristie Dean

My healing hands showed themselves in my early teenage years. I believe all things happen for a reason in life, good and bad. I know that as the sexual abuse definitely awakened me instantly to my surroundings, forcing me in many ways to find and heal feelings inside my mind and body. This was a result of the tension and stress of living with my abuser over so many years and never having a moment to forget what had happened, forced to face it every day.

I know that stress, tension, and uncertainty affects your body. I was feeling tense all the time, picking up illnesses easily, and my body was always aching. I'd spend a lot of hours on my bed contemplating life and the **space** around me, trying to find a better way to survive the days without everything overwhelming me. That taught me to always try to pick yourself up and be positive and motivated as best you can, and deal with what you've got in life. It definitely takes you to a different level of understanding about everything.

Not only that, but that little girl inside me had a lot of anger. I know that nothing could have hurt me more than that sexual abuse, and the constant verbal, and even physical abuse that I had around me. It made me act very tough and strong, nothing really fazed me. I was a bit of a bully, always having my guard up and ready to tell anyone off who I didn't agree with. I know now that I was **protecting** myself.

Around this time, I went to my first healer and message therapist mentor, Jill. She was soon teaching me different ways to release and let go of pain in my body. Jill always worked intuitively and guided from the heart, and worked with healing spirits. Working with her and spending time with her resonated with me, and I could feel the instant changes it was having on my body. I realised there was more than just a massage going on here. Jill would often work with crystals on different parts of my body. I could actually feel the connection to spirit and release a lot of the tension in my body.

My relationship with Jill went on for years, learning more and more from her. She taught me Touch for Health, and how to do body muscle testing. It was hands-on healing work using spiritual energies to guide you in helping clients. Sometimes I would double up with her on clients, helping her connect and using my own intuition to help heal and give relief and **guidance** to them. I remember one day Jill taking me to Karratha, an hour away. We arrived at a caravan park that had a recreational centre, and met up with a group of all different healers. It was a healing day for healers, so there were about 15-20 other people there. I was the youngest. The healers pulled out massage tables, and everyone was assigned to work with somebody. This was all interesting to me, and I remember the power of this day vividly.

There was powerful stuff going on in the room. There was talk about people having internal operations all done spiritually, on the massage table. I can remember one particular male healer working on me, and I could feel him accessing different parts of my body just using his mind and his hands. It was a little hard to explain; it wasn't the conventional healing where you go to a doctor and get a pill for some symptoms, or you have an operation. This was at a completely different level, and no doubt that it was just as powerful.

When we were about to leave, Jill was talking to a lady just outside the recreational centre. I asked her what she'd done to her head, as she had a bump and a cut. Jill interrupted me and said, 'Kristie, this lady's third eye has been opening up'. She had been working intensely with somebody who had been in intensive care, and she was going to the hospital daily and working alongside the patient with deep spiritual healing. She told me the work was so intense that it had actually opened her third eye up. I didn't really understand at the time; I was young and didn't have the spiritual level of understanding, but I could feel the energy and power of those people. I knew that they were all sincere, and that what they were telling me was their actual experiences. It just wasn't your everyday teenage **conversation** or event that you would see. It was very special for me to have witnessed this at such a young age.

Going into my late teenage years, I was known in my town for my own massage healing work. I treated it as a hobby because it was a passion, and it was all word of mouth. I actually did some really good work in that time, and I thought it was very cool. When I turned 21 I had that huge birthday party in town, and a whole group of my friends put in and bought me my first massage table, one I still have now. It's pink and I'm very proud of it; it's done a lot of traveling and healing work over the years.

My hands, mind, and spirit just started guiding me with massage, and I was helping heal other people's bodies as well as my own. I'm not quite sure how it happened, but I started to manipulate my own, and others' backs and necks. I don't know where this came from, other than the fact that I'd been in quite a few car accidents by the time I was 21 and I had loose ligaments in my neck, so I was often cracking it to give myself relief. Some people would cringe when they'd see me do it, but it felt good.

Soon I was asked by people to help them with their back and neck to straighten them out, and I would manipulate them like a chiropractor would. I knew that this could be dangerous and strange, but people would ask me to do it. All I can say is luckily I never hurt anyone or did any damage – it's only ever helped heal and relieve pain and tension. It wasn't unusual in my teenage years to be at the pub and have a few of the guys and girls laying on the floor, offering me $5 if I would click their back in. It was hilarious, and very entertaining for everyone.

Getting my **massage** table is still one of the best things I've ever received as a present. It travelled everywhere with me in my 20s, to lots of different towns. It's been around Australia a couple of times, and it always popped out every now and then to give relief to people on my journeys. It was a natural talent that I had, something I have always felt very comfortable doing, almost as if I had lived other lives doing this healing work. It feels like it's in my soul. Using my healing hands always made me feel so energised, and was when I was happiest.

I have dedicated this book to Jill because she was my first healing mentor, and some of the things that she taught me in those early years guided me into my path of learning and healing, as I've done many different studies and learning modalities since then. I lost contact with Jill from the age of 21 until the end of 2016. We have found each other again, and it feels like we picked up where we left off. Our **friendship** and connection has been one of the deepest I have ever felt in life. While writing this book she has spiritually healed some of the subconscious energies that came up for me, which improved my body and helped me find the strength to tell my raw, but real life stories, turning my hurt into power.

Listen, Act, and Survive

*'You are here to enable the divine **purpose** of the universe to unfold. That is how important you are!'*

– Eckhart Tolle

Or should I say flight, fright, or freeze? As if I didn't have enough going on in my life, between the ages of 14 to 19 I was involved in two major car rollovers that left the cars demolished, and a third car accident where I was lucky I wasn't cut in half.

The first car accident happened in the early 1980s, when I was still living in Wickham. A girlfriend of mine asked me to go on a family trip with her, her mother, and her sister. The plan was to buy some presents to send back with her grandparents to Slovakia after their visit to Australia. If we wanted to do any decent shopping we needed to drive to Port Hedland, as our small mining town didn't have much in the way of shopping facilities. This was common for people in Wickham to travel the two and a half hours just to do their big shopping, anything other than food.

My girlfriend's mother said it wasn't a good day from the beginning; she felt uneasy, but the trip had to go ahead. We had done our shopping and all the things that we needed to do, and we were on our way home, but my girlfriend's mother was still feeling off. She kept telling us to fasten our seatbelts, and she was keeping to the speed limit of 100km. We stopped at Windy Creek, the halfway mark on our trip home. We needed some petrol and some cold drinks, and my girlfriend's mother decided to **check the tyres**. She reminded us when we got back in the car to put on our seatbelts as we were distracted listening to our Walkman, playing music and giggling, and telling stories.

My girlfriend and I were both sitting in the backseat, and her sister, Tanya, was in the front in a booster seat, as she was only four years old. Approximately 7km out of Roebourne, the car struck a rock on the side of the road. It lodged between the rim and the tyre and pushed the tyre off. The steering wheel was violently ripped out of my friend's mum's hands and the car pulled left and locked up. There was absolutely no control over the car. Everything was moving in slow motion.

These moments in life have never, ever left me. I could feel my heart racing faster, and every muscle in my body becoming tense. I could feel my pupils dilating; my body was going into the fight, flight, or freeze response. There was a whole monologue going on in my head as these seconds passed, though it seemed like twenty minutes. I was thinking, 'Oh my God, this is it – I've lived my life already and I'm going to die'. It was as if I could feel the end of my life was here, and I was witnessing it. I was feeling pissed off and angry, thinking that I want the power to live longer than this, surely this can't be all it is. I was thinking of my family and loved ones as my whole life was flashing and smashing in front of me.

The car rolled five times across the open, dry, red dirt field, and stopped partly on the roof, and then rolled back onto the side. It felt as if I was watching a movie in slow motion with me in it. It was a complete out-of-body experience. The car stopped. I was alive. I could see blood everywhere. I remember looking around to see where everyone was, and making sure we were all okay. I **believe** we'd all gone into a fright, flight, and freeze response. We were all then wandering around in the desert with no shoes on, wondering where we are. No one could speak. This went on for quite a few minutes. The shock had just frozen us all speechless at first. We could all see each other and see that we were alive, but it took minutes before we could respond verbally to each other.

We eventually gathered ourselves and knew that we needed to get help, but we were on an isolated road. It probably took thirty or so minutes before a car passed us and saw the destruction. There were pieces of the car laying kilometres away. The two year old Cortina was now in parts. We had an ambulance there soon, and we were all taken to hospital. Miraculously, we had only cuts and bruises. My feet were burnt from the heat coming off the ground. I'd lost my shoes in the tumble.

As a result of this experience, for quite a few years afterwards I was a very nervous passenger in a car. I went through a phase when driving with my mum on dirt roads where if the car ever felt out of control I would burst out crying and screaming. But over the next few years I had to live through it and push beyond it, because as I was getting closer to turning 17 I wanted my own driver's license. I needed to be in control of the car, as I felt more vulnerable when someone else was driving.

It was all a simple psychological effect, and I was **determined** to fight these fears. Stupidly enough, it didn't stop me from getting into cars with my friends before we were 17. We would go out on dirt roads and push the limits by performing hand brakes on the loose gravel. We would have the music blaring, Cold Chisel piercing our ears. We got off on risking our lives, and I really can't believe we used to do it. We were crazy kids of the '80s. Little did I know that in just a couple of years after that full-on car accident, I would be in my second rollover.

I was 16. One of my girlfriends who I grew up with was a year older than me, but because she'd come over from England it meant we were in the same year at school. For her this was cool as she got her driver's license before me. She was excited because her father had been working on a car for her that he'd bought, completely stripping it to bare bones and putting it back together from scratch. I remember seeing him working on it in their driveway, for months on end. It was a love job for him, creating his eldest daughter's first car. He was tremendously proud of it.

My girlfriend finally got her license, after many attempts, mind you. She took possession of the car her father had been building for her, and that was a special moment between father and daughter. This one beautiful summer day we decided to go joyriding, so we went a few kilometres out onto dirt tracks near the local rubbish tip. We thought this was a great place for her to practice her new driving skills and go zooming around. I'm sure we would have had loud music playing, probably Cold Chisel again.

The windows were down as it was a reasonably warm day. I had my arm out the window, holding onto the roof of the car with my hand, being a real cool cat. It was also a way of grabbing on tight as we would be cruising around the corners, sliding sideways on the loose gravel. Unexpectedly, she lost control. We went up an embankment, rolled. I can remember everything **slowing down**. Our bodies violently tumbled in the car, going around and around. My heart was racing again, and my pupils dilating – everything that I felt before was happening again, the slow motion, life flashing before me. It was déjà vu.

The car rolled 3-4 times. 'Oh damn, not again,' I was thinking, but amazingly enough, and miracle number two, I was alive, and so was my girlfriend. The details afterwards weren't as clear as the first car accident I was in, but the things I do remember was looking down at my three fingers that I'd had hanging out of the car, crushed in the accident – the car had literally rolled over my fingers. Most of my fingers were mangled, hanging onto bone, but I couldn't feel pain, and that surprised me. It didn't seem real that I was looking down at my own hand. I guess it happened so quickly and my body protected me from the pain. My girlfriend gathered herself after realising she was fine, and realised **action needed** to be taken. She took her top off and wrapped it round my hand to stop the bleeding, leaving her in a bikini top and shorts. The car was completely totalled. 'Wow, we did a good job of that one,' we said to each other as we looked in complete disbelief.

My girlfriend was amazing; she took complete control of me, knowing that I was the one who needed the help. We were off the beaten track and there were no cars to get help. My girlfriend gathered me and we walked off to find one of the main roads to alert some help. I remember us having to walk for about half an hour before we got onto a road where we knew cars would be coming past. **Eventually** a guy stopped in his car, although he really didn't understand why we are walking along in our bikinis with my hand wrapped up. He didn't realised that we had just been in a major car rollover, because the car wasn't visible by now.

I can remember his disbelief that we were demanding to go to the hospital as quickly as possible, but after we explained, he trusted us and took us straight there. I still couldn't feel the pain yet, but it wasn't long until it kicked in. Once we got to the hospital and the doctors had a look at my hand, my body went into complete shock. This was another complete out-of-body experience. I could see everyone around me, hear the doctors, the panic. I could feel the tremendous pain in my hand and fingers; it was excruciating.

But I couldn't talk, and my body wouldn't move. I completely froze up. My fingers were a complete mess, and there wasn't a doctor who could even deal with this situation in my town. The closest doctor on duty was in Roebourne, 12km away, so they took me in the ambulance. I could see everything happening around me, but I couldn't respond. I couldn't lift my legs or my arms an inch. I was actually trying to, but my body was just not responding. I remember being very fascinated by this, but confused, and very worried. I guess that's what you call shock and fear. My mind couldn't cope with what it was seeing and feeling. It was just profound.

Within a couple of days, I was flown down to Perth to a specialist plastic surgeon. There was no way that they had specialists in the Pilbara who could handle that. In a few days, I had my first surgery. Because I'd lost so much of one of my fingers, they attached one of my fingers to the other finger so that it could **grow together** for a few weeks and get some more flesh around it. After the operation, they wrapped my hand up in hard plaster cast and bandages. I looked like a Dalek out of *Dr* Who, and I remember for weeks I couldn't put my arms straight down – it had to stay up because of the pressure that it would cause if I put my arm down.

My girlfriends came and stayed with me in those two weeks between the operations, so it was like we were on holidays together. We had so much fun, and because I couldn't eat properly, let alone dress myself, my girlfriends all helped; putting dresses on, going shopping. We were hanging out down in Bunbury along the beach coast, meeting lots of boys. I actually fell in love that summer, even with my hand all wrapped up. My spirit always shone brightly and I stayed positive – it's helped me through many things in my life – so when I look back, despite the major accident, I remember that summer because I fell in love with a guy, and I had the most awesome time with my girlfriends.

I had more passion in my heart after surviving that car accident again, as opposed to being depressed about the fact that I'd lost a couple ends of my fingers that required reconstruction. I look back at that young teenager and say, 'Well done, Kristie. You kept yourself strong and **positive**'. I wouldn't have changed a thing. I had the second operation where they detached my fingers and then they grew freely, and there were lots of painful stitches to be removed. Remarkably, my fingernails grew back. After all these years, I almost forget what happened to my fingers. It hasn't affected me, as I have full function of my hand, and my fingers being damaged has never really held me back.

My philosophy was, 'Get on with it and don't think about it – move forward and be strong'. I just didn't dwell on things. I got my driver's license just two weeks after I turned 17, so now I was in control, and I think I always felt better about that. I've always looked back at this experience and being surprised on how shock took over my body, but also as such a fond, amazing event to have experienced as a human.

My third accident occurred when I was 19. I was on my way to work at the day-care centre, driving a white and brown two-tone Holden Kingswood, my first car. There are only a few main streets in Wickham, and the centre is in the heart of the town. I had been working there for a year by now. It was 7:00am and I had just indicated to turn into the next main street. Boom. Huge smash. The side of my car was hit, the full impact on my driver's door, and I was smashed viciously through the fence around our local fire station. The car stopped, and I know that I'd indicated because I could hear the indicator and see still the light flickering. This was not like the other car accidents where time stood still; this happened so quickly. A 4WD had attempted to take me over at the intersection. It was completely his fault.

The driver in the other car came to see if I was okay and helped me out of the car. I was in one piece but the driver door was smashed in, pushing up on my legs, so I had to escape out of the passenger door. The other driver quickly fled the scene, and was nowhere to be seen when the police came. I **have suspicions** that the driver wasn't sober, even though it was early in the morning. I was lucky my legs weren't crushed, as the whole impact was on the driver's door. I was only centimetres from **losing** my legs.

I initiated court proceedings with the other driver for costs. I was a determined, strong 19 year old, and he was not getting away with it. Even though he didn't turn up to court a few times and tried everything to stop the proceedings, I stuck to my guns and eventually he paid. I'm also very happy to report that I've never been in a car accident in the 26 years since then.

Sisterly Love

a reflection by Cherie Nielsen

For our friendship to have endured from childhood to middle-age, I think it is a testament to how special our bond is. Although not my biological sister, I am proud to call this gorgeous woman my spiritual/soulmate sister. Kristie is a kindred spirit and someone I have been drawn to since our childhood days in the Pilbara. I, a publican's daughter, and Kristie, the daughter of a mine worker, we could not have come from more polar opposite home lives. Whilst mine was carefree, Kristie's, although loving and welcoming (beautiful mother, and annoying, but loveable, little brothers), it was tainted by trouble within.

*This emotional turmoil would, at times, manifest itself through Kristie's hair trigger reactions. There were many confrontations with other girls, mainly from other towns, and usually because of boys – their boys' interest in us! Kristie was one tough chick and could certainly hold her own, but if the numbers were unfair then I'd have her back, as she would and does for me to this very day. Underneath all that bravado was a beautiful, kind-hearted kid, an **absolute diamond** in the Pindan rough.*

Many an adventure has been shared from the north-west to the big smoke, and further down to the south-west of WA. Summer holidays were spent in Bunbury, staying with Nanna and Pop Deans at their retirement village. It wasn't uncommon for us to wake up startled (after being out until the wee hours and looking very much the worse for wear) with Nanna standing in our bedroom doorway with a gathering of delightfully wrinkle-faced ladies, proudly pointing out her 'lovely granddaughter and her little friend'. Nanna and Pop were so very proud of their golden-haired girl, Kristie. As teenagers, we thought ourselves Pilbara-tough – girls who could handle dirt bikes, not take shit from anyone, and participate in our sporting endeavours in the searing heat.

However, that didn't necessarily translate to city suaveness. As effortless as it may appear to cross a busy city street or climb aboard an escalator, these everyday activities could be very challenging for the uninitiated, and I am proud to say that once I became a city slicker I was able to pass on my expertise on these monumental life challenges to my dear friend, Kristie.

I believe that our friendship has been cemented by our shared personality traits. We both have a crazy, and sometimes inappropriate sense of humour. Kristie has the loudest, most infectious of laughs, and that is totally in line with her loud and infectious personality. We are bonded further by the fact that we both definitely carry the gene attributed to wild and, at times, naughty side of our personality. After one particularly big night out, poor Kristie woke up in my bed very worried, saying, '**Surely not**, there is no way!' We were very relieved that the water beneath her was only a leak in my waterbed, caused by Kimmy the cat!

One could not ask for a more reliable and loyal friend than Kristie. She is a second daughter to my parents, Tim and Dee, and is adored by my son, Ethan. The **strength and longevity** of our friendship is testament to *our deep respect for one another that only strengthens with each passing year. Even when faced with those most challenging of life's obstacles, and no matter how dark the days, Kristie's tenacity and positivity still shines brightly outwards from deep within. She is a friend who will carry you in times of darkness, and laugh with you until you cry in the happiest of times. She is a remarkably strong individual who is an inspiration to myself and many women.*

*I am so very proud of you, my gorgeous girl, for everything that you have **achieved** and everything that you are yet to achieve. Love you heaps.*

Moving and Thriving

'Where there is **great love**, there are always miracles.'

– Willa Cather

Full of energy, I had a huge desire for bigger dreams, more possibilities, and more options. It was time for me to get the hell out of that small mining town and actually experience the world. By 21, I'd become one of the local drug masterminds in the town. I knew how to bring in pounds of marijuana, how to bury it and hide it, how to weigh it up, how to safely distribute it, how to work it smart, and how not to be caught.

I learnt all these things because that's what had surrounded me most of my life. It was almost like I was being groomed for the position; if that's what you hear and see for most of your life, that's what you become. I was very good at it, but it was time for me to get out of this situation. I was smart enough to know that who I was came from what I knew, and I wanted to know more. Both my parents had moved over to Bundaberg in Queensland, so I knew that this was my chance to experience the world and leave the mining town behind.

I was so excited and passionate about this change that people could feel it around me, so much so that a few of my friends in Wickham decided to take the journey with me, to open up their minds to new **possibilities.** There were four of us all up, three other girlfriends and a male friend. We flew from Karratha down to Perth, and then over to Queensland. This was exciting and scary for us, because we'd all grown up in the country mining town and had never even lived anywhere where there were traffic lights before. I remember how funny it was when we would walk down the street in Bundaberg and say, 'Hi, how are you today?' to everyone I made eye-contact with. I could tell the locals were finding this quite strange. But I grew up in a small mining town where we all knew each other, so for me it was normal. I guess you could say I was a bit of a Crocodile Dundee in the big smoke.

Over the next few years, I certainly made my presence felt in Queensland. I studied many different things; my beauty therapy certificate, tourism and hospitality, and I worked in lots of different restaurants and nightclubs, and just about every pub in town. My heart was full of excitement, and I just wanted to learn and experience it all, so I tried everything that I possibly could. I worked in Sportsgirl where I broke quite a few records during my time. I just loved working in sales, and with people.

Another job that I made a real mark in was in sales working for Austar, a pay TV company in the country. I was working mostly with men in a small team. We all had our own territories to work in and I loved this, always finding new and innovative ways to work my area. Day in and day out I'd be one of the first back in the office, having already made my sales for the day. A lot of the guys couldn't **believe it** – this cute little blonde girl with lots of energy who would always come in with more sales than all of the guys who had been in the industry for a few years.

But I always had a goal to work smart, not hard, and work faster and quicker to get the results. I had my own little marketing system set up for myself, and I had stickers of myself plastered all over my marketing material when I would hit a territory. This would all be direct door-to-door sales. I'd be so full of enthusiasm that my energy was contagious. I usually left houses feeling excited about getting their pay TV and the satellite dish put on their home. I was good at having **an answer** – I could sell ice to an Eskimo. But I did it with real passion and authenticity, and I had a natural ability to build rapport with people.

I'd been dating a guy for over a year at this point, and we decided to plan a trip around Australia. He had purchased a new caravan for us, a brand new 4WD, and we had matching bikes; every little thing you could imagine a young couple would ever dream about having to travel around Australia. It was very exciting. A few months before we were meant to be heading off, I met another man and fell in love. We'd met working together in a sports club, and it just happened. Being an open and honest person, I had to come forward to my boyfriend and tell him that I had feelings for someone else, and that I was confused. In the end, I decided that I was going to set my feelings aside for this other guy and stick to my plans of travelling around Australia with my boyfriend, as we had planned it for a long time and he'd understood and accepted that we needed to give it a chance.

I refocussed my **concentration** with my boyfriend and we started our trip. We headed up the Queensland coast and stopped at Darwin, where we both worked for nearly four months. Darwin was an amazing place; it had an energy, a feeling about it – somewhere that felt like home, where you wanted to stay and explore. I worked in a private childcare centre there for a few months and that was very stimulating, and it gave me money to travel on.

We drove across Northern Territory and down the Western Australian coast, and then ended up back in Wickham. My partner was a carpenter and he was offered contract work on some of the housing in the town, as it all needed upgrading. This was a huge opportunity for him, and very **financially lucrative**. I found myself working back in the same childcare centre as before. As exciting as it was travelling around Australia, I felt stuck again. I remember having a lot of dreams reflecting this feeling. I guess you could say I just never really felt settled there again, even though a lot of people were living there who I had grown up with, and known for most of my life.

It was quite a coincidence that we had our caravan parked in a friend's property in Wickham, and the caravan was parked right up by the fence next door to the property where I had lived many years before. This caravan was parked right next to my old caravan that I'd bought when I was 20 because I'd planned to go around Australia, and was living in it. It was symbolic that three years later, in a brand new caravan with my then-partner, I lived within touching distance of the caravan I once dreamed about driving around Australia in. It was a bit surreal, seeing the two caravans sitting side-by-side.

It symbolised a lot of growth and change within myself, however, I was slowly growing frustrated, and also had a lot of thoughts about the other man back in Queensland. I had strong feelings for him and my heart still pulled me back. I would sneak phone calls and letters to him, so this was definitely not a **healthy situation** for the partner that I was actually with at the time. I came clean, told him how I felt, and decided to leave him. He continued to live there for nearly seven years.

I moved down to Perth for a while, and spent some time living with my newly-discovered sister – a half-sister, my mother's first born. Nicole is 18 months older than I am, born when my mother was only 15 years old. Because of my mother's age, her baby was taken away from her. I spent about six months there, learning more about my sister, her husband, and her history. Bonding with her wasn't difficult because the power of genes was just so strong between us. We were very similar and we would think the same way often, so we both found those months together very amusing. Still, in all this time, the guy from Queensland was still in my heart. We were calling each other regularly, so I felt drawn back to Queensland to meet up again, and see where my life could go. Perth gave me the time with my sister to get to know her, but also to have the space between my two lovers to help my heart decide between them.

My parents were both still living in Bundaberg so I found myself boarding at home again. I'd reunited with my love from work, Patrick, and he became my boyfriend for many years after that. My relationship with Pat was strong. We were both very much in love, and we had a lot in common. We were both very spiritual; we loved meditating and sharing **spiritual experiences** together. We also enjoyed doing positive motivational mind courses, and we were often off learning something. We also had an interest in sales; he had his own company that he was trying to get going.

Pat was in my life to show me how I was meant to be loved, and I really felt a profound heart connection. When I was around 24 years old, Patrick and I were doing a lot of meditation together. We would meet up with another lady and do deep meditations together, and also some psychometrics and different spiritual experiences. But even with all this mental, positive excitement that I had in my life, my body was always struggling physically. I'd spend a lot of my early 20s with a lot of migraines and suffered really badly with them. I knew that my immune system and my **strength** could have been stronger. I still had massage clients who I would work with during that time, but what I learnt was that I needed to work on releasing and letting go of some of my own problems.

Releasing and Letting Go

'There are some things I'd like to say to you. Allow me the voice to **express** myself. I will support you. You will have abundance and you will have love.'

– Patrick Pope

I knew I needed to let go of the heavyweight burden of the horrible, soul-sucking secret of the sexual abuse that silenced me at nine years old. I had no way of voicing my experience, and was supressed beyond belief. I knew this because I was doing a lot of meditation, and I could feel some of those suppressed feelings coming up. I wanted to be in better health, so I needed to face the truth and let it out of my body.

With the true support of Patrick, by talking about how I was feeling and holding the space for me through meditation and **unconditional love**, I know that I was guided to where it was time for me to face my father and my mother, and talk about the sexual abuse. I just wanted to be free of the heaviness, and I knew that I deserved to be free inside myself; to clear that block inside of me and be as healthy as I could be. I was still suffering with debilitating migraines, and I knew that my body could be a lot healthier and stronger.

This energy inside me was holding me to ransom, and I was intent on dealing with it. I provoked this dark, suppressed energy and the emotions rose as if it had happened yesterday. I allowed my mind to go there, something I had not permitted all those years. This was one of the most powerful physical and mental experiences of my life. It was time to give myself permission to stand up for the violation.

I approached my parents and told them the story. My father had never denied what had happened, and could see that I was a complete mess. Just bringing it up made it very difficult to breathe, let alone to speak fully about it. My body was completely broken. In the hours after telling my parents we were all a complete mental mess. We all cried, but it was very difficult for my mum to believe and she denied it for a days; that was just her coping mechanism, I believe. It was very hard for me to hear that she wasn't sure that she believed my story. That added to the trauma.

Over the **next week** or so, I just cried my eyes out. I found it difficult to walk; I was in extreme pain. But I knew I needed to go through this and feel the emotions, to physically get the painful energy out of my body. It had been held inside all these years – the violation of the sexual abuse and having to live with it in my family. It was all about releasing and letting go, not about pointing a finger at my father or trying to destroy him. It was about **forgiveness**, so that I could ultimately live a healthier and freer life inside my body. I can remember at one stage the three of us didn't know what to do with ourselves. We were all so emotionally wrecked that we almost needed to call in reinforcements for support, but it was so personal and raw that we managed to get through it, and over hours and days, we did.

I needed the space from my parents and was staying at my boyfriend's house, and he was supporting me as it took more than a week to get the crying, pain, and exhaustion out of my body. One late evening I was still crying, and it was just unstoppable. I went out to the big backyard of the property to feel the fresh air. I bent down on my knees in prayer position, because I actually didn't have the energy to stand anymore, and I cried and screamed and yelled so hard and so powerfully to remove the energy held inside me. It was like an exorcism, pushing and screaming the pain from deep inside me. I felt 100% better, probably better than I had in my life. It was a massive, unbelievable release. After going through that, I could see the steps that I needed to take to be **much stronger** and be more directed in my life.

Releasing and Letting Go

Still living in Bundaberg and dating Patrick, an opportunity arose for us to undertake a month-long project together in Townsville. We were asked to put together and manage a direct sales territory for a company called Telesavers, contracted to Telstra. This was very exciting for both Patrick and I as we were highly motivated people together, and thought of working together would be awesome. We arranged to stay in a caravan park in the town, so our first step was to advertise in the local paper for direct sales people to help us with our project.

We needed people to work door-to-door and hit certain areas in Townsville, offering Telstra clients products, adding ones direct to their homes, and also great discounts for their phone services. We had to get people who were interested in working on a commission basis, so they were only paid for the contracts and the work that they put in. We knew that this would be a challenge. Our ad attracted more than 150 people who we scaled down to two teams of about 30. Patrick was to run one team externally from the caravan park and I was running the other from inside, which I called the 'caravan park team'. We'd **broken down** the territory that we needed to cover in Townsville and had our goals set for numbers that we wanted to achieve.

The project was a huge success. My team was mostly filled with backpackers travelling around Australia. Most of them had decided to move into the same caravan park where we were living to make it easier. Patrick was running his team from a local McDonald's, and I was holding my morning sales training in the barbecue areas, so for weeks you would see backpackers creeping out of their tents in their suits for meetings. I was a cute, petite blonde who loved her business outfits, and especially her shoes. I can only imagine how entertaining we must have been for the other residents – a whole bunch of backpackers with this young blonde girl running the show. Hilarious!

The energy and excitement was amazing; the direct sales teams were making a lot of **money,** averaging $700-$1000 per week. per person. We created a rivalry between the two teams so they'd compete with the amount of sales at the end of the day. Patrick and I had a small cabin-style accommodation in the caravan park, so of an evening we would set up a table at the front door and all the contractors would drop off their work and contracts from the day. Patrick and I would add them all up and work out how much we owed them for the day.

This project was the second time Patrick and I had worked together. In the first six weeks, we broke records in the industry. Our sales rates within that timeframe hadn't been done before. The word got out nationally in the telecommunications industry. People from the company had flown up to Townsville to do a big presentation to our two groups and we were given a huge sales trophy and recognition for the work we'd done. After we successfully completed the Townsville project, Patrick and I drove back home to Bundaberg. We started to think about the opportunities that we could have working together, getting our own contracts direct with Telstra or other communications companies. We were a powerhouse working together; Patrick was the analytical/figures man, setting all the goals up and directing us in that way, and I was the people-person, very good at training and motivating. **Together**, we knew that we could to make it.

We decided to leave Bundaberg. I bought a trailer and we filled it with our belongings, off to Sydney to hit the big time for ourselves. We wanted to utilise the fact that word had got out about the project in the telecommunications industry, and we knew that could give us some leverage to go directly to the large companies, and not be contracted to one. Within a short period of time, Patrick and I had weaved ourselves through the industry and found ourselves with our first major national contract with AAPT. We formed a company called Insight Visions New Age Marketing. I called my brother, Jay, who was still living in the Pilbara. He was only in his early teens and he had lost direction and hadn't found what he wanted to do with his life. I knew that our personalities were quite similar and that he would thrive off sales and marketing.

I got him a plane ticket and brought him over to Sydney. He rocked up with long hair, a beard, and a suitcase of minimal clothes that consisted of black t-shirts and shorts – he was in a bit of a dark place. We scrubbed him up, bought him his first suit, and from that moment on his life changed. His beard came off, his hair got shorter, and the suit stayed on. He worked with us for years after that, as he followed us through many different contracts and states around Australia. We were running three states and covering huge areas of direct sales. After winding up our contract with AAPT, we were then given the **opportunity** to pitch to Optus. Again, a huge success. Our company became one of the first two direct sales companies to take Optus pay TV and telecommunications externally. This was a huge achievement because up until that point Optus controlled all of their own internal sales teams.

We were living in Vulture Street in Brisbane, near the Gabba, and we had our Insight Visions office in the Fortitude Valley. This way we could have close access to the Optus buildings and work directly with them, and get the results we needed. It was a truly inspiring time in my life. I was positive and motivating; I had to get results out of big teams and I did it with passion and conviction. After this project we decided to move to Melbourne with another contract, taking a different direction. We started working with a company called Australian Star Communications.

Over the years I had the opportunity to work and train with some of the best in the industry. I spent a lot of time with a man called Sandy MacGregor. Sandy's teaching helped me hugely in the '90s. He taught creative accelerated learning methods, and scientifically-proven techniques that would unleash 80% of the power of your amazing mind. He taught me how to relax my mind and **release stress** in 30 seconds, and helped increase my memory and recall by focusing concentration to easily expand the use of my mind. He helped me to achieve my goals faster and enhance my life skills. He also taught me to access the meditative state very quickly to direct and focus the power of the subconscious mind.

I later went on to do his Train the Trainer course in the Blue Mountains, and that gave me vital skills to become a better facilitator and help me teach and train my teams, learning to get the most out of them, and to achieve their personal goals, too. All his insights and strengths helped me to achieve the goals we set for Insight Visions Marketing. Sandy wrote the bestselling book *Piece of Mind*, and several other books including *Students Steps to Success* that has been endorsed by many top educators. He also wrote *Switch on to Your Inner Strength*, and made a difference to thousands of Australians and New Zealanders. He conducted training seminars and talks in Australia to the public education corporate sectors. He was my idol and mentor throughout much of the '90s, and I pay honour to him here.

I also was incredibly lucky to meet motivational speaker Denis Waitley more than 20 years ago, and found him to be a very profound man. Before this happened, I had focussed my thoughts on meeting him, visualizing it, and had even planned what question I would ask him. I went to a huge entertainment centre in Brisbane with Patrick to hear him and many other amazing **inspirational speakers**. After he finished there was an intermission. I was torn between needing to go to the toilet and running to the stage to try meet Denis. I decided the toilet needed my immediate attention, so I took off in a huge rush, pulling Patrick with me though the huge crowds. Suddenly, in what I say was a huge crowd of probably 20,000 people, I landed in the arms of Mr Denis Waitley! In complete disbelief, I apologised for almost bumping him off his feet backwards, and was so eager to ask my question.

'Well,' he said, 'you had better ask me then.'

'If you could advise me to read any book in the world, what would it be?' I asked.

He answered, *'The Bible.'*

I thanked him and parted with a big smile, amazed at the power of my mind and how thoughts can manifest and attract things into your life. I have experienced this hundreds of times throughout my amazing life since then, so dream and believe in the power within you. If phones had a camera back then and weren't the size of a brick, I'm sure we would have had a selfie together!

At the end of 1999 I was offered a job in Perth. I felt drawn back there and was excited to be around more friends and family. Even though the last four years of running my own company was amazing, and the highlights and achievements were incredible, there was something I was still struggling with inside me; my body seemed to be getting weaker. I went from a girl who was very fit and strong to someone who was slowly putting a bit of weight on, unable to **exercise** the way that I had before.

I started getting more and more headaches, but I couldn't work out what was wrong with me. I was spending a lot of time at the doctor getting blood tests because I felt like

I had a virus that was not going away. I had a very strong mind to achieve things, but physically my body was letting me down. It was a very confusing time. This was putting a lot of pressure on Patrick, because he couldn't understand how this strong girl was feeling ill all the time and was physically unable to cope. At times, I thought that maybe I was just unfit, and I had to push myself harder. I'd ask, 'Why is it that I go for a half hour walk and I have to stop intermittently, in pain?'

Feeling so unwell physically started to take a mental toll. I remember feeling **frustrated** and very angry with myself, because this is not who I wanted to be; the girl I was was sliding down the pole.

Insight Visions

a reflection by Patrick Pope

Kristie had ambition and drive to succeed in her chosen field of marketing. She built teams that fed off each other's **enthusiasm**, rousing them to compete in a friendly rivalry that spurred success and recognition as a group on a national basis.

Kristie was a good leader. She oozed passion and was inspiring. She had focus, confidence, was open-minded, positive and decisive, fair and persistent. She was always accountable, and a great organiser. Most importantly, but maybe the least recognised quality in modern society, she is/was highly intuitive.

From a small pilot project gathering 30 backpackers into a caravan park, to at one stage running a team of more than 120 door-to-door salespeople across three states, her passion and belief in others helped them achieve their own unmatched success. **This journey** took her to Sydney, Brisbane, Melbourne, and then Perth. Each step saw a growth in self-confidence and self-awareness.

Even though her company at the time had no 'history', what gained the attention of the marketing managers and directors of these companies was her belief in herself, her team, and the products these companies had to offer the public and business sectors. Belief in self coupled with passion, desire, and persistence were the magnets to attract into her life what the universe had **destined**.

All experiences a human moves through has brought them to this moment. love yourself, and you will discover true freedom.

Anne Akers

The CML Bomb

'When I **let go** of what I am, I become what I might be.'

– Laozi

At 7:00am on 23 October 2000, I woke up feeling pissed off. I had hardly slept during the night, and the little sleep I did have seemed to have taken me into a crazy dream state that felt like a nightmare. It was those dreams where you feel like you've been battling yourself, trying to survive, and everything's a struggle so you wake up feeling like you haven't been asleep at all; you've been up all night fighting battles in your mind. Lately it had been normal to wake up tired, aching, and grumpy.

I told Patrick about my horrible dreams and my bad sleep, and that must have been quite depressing for him, so I picked up my dream book from the bedside table to look at what my dream meant. It always told me the same thing: your body is not well. I was so pissed off that I threw the book across the room, just missing Pat (I wasn't aiming for him!). I've always been aware of my dreams and they've often given me good **guidance** in my life, but I wasn't getting the answers I wanted to hear.

Pat ignored my attitude and went to work. Just as it hit 8:00, the phone rang. I thought that was strange, as it was a bit early for a call. It was the receptionist at the doctor's surgery asking me to come in to discuss the results of some tests I had taken earlier. The receptionist insisted that I bring someone close to me for moral support, as I would be getting some results that I may be more comfortable sharing with somebody. I became quite stressed and asked for the results right then, but they explained that it was policy to **book an appointment** so the doctor could discuss it with me. I was booked in for 9:00.

After putting the phone down, I immediately jumped in the shower because I really needed to wake up and get some hot water on my body, as it was aching all over. My thoughts were racing – what was going on? It had been years now that my body had been breaking down, and I was exhausted. I wanted answers, so there was a part of me that was excited to get the answers I'd been wanting for years.

I called my mum, who was now also living in Perth, and explained to her about the phone call, and if she would please come with me as Patrick was at work. My mum didn't hesitate, and was at my house as soon as possible. She was stressed out and upset that I wasn't getting answers for my poor health. My mum drove us to the appointment; I would not have been well enough to drive the car myself. We chatted the whole way there, though my mind was racing. Mum was trying to keep me calm, and herself, too.

Dr Wendy Stokes was my new doctor, and I had only just been referred to her as I wasn't getting **results** anywhere else. When we sat I said, 'Okay, so what's wrong with me?'

'Kristie,' Dr Stokes said. 'We have the results of your blood test. You have leukaemia.'

I didn't know what that meant exactly, but I knew that it was cancer, so the first words out of my mouth were, 'Why the fuck wasn't I told this earlier?' I became very angry because my search for this result had lasted years, and I didn't understand why I was only getting a result now. Dr Stokes calmed me down, understanding that this news was not good. She couldn't give me many answers other than that I needed to get more tests done so that we could figure out where to go from there.

She did explain that the type of cancer I had was called Chronic Myeloid Leukaemia (CML). This type of cancer is normally found in patients through blood tests, and most of the time they don't have any symptoms so are unaware that they even have the disease. My case was different as I had been struggling physically for years. She explained that the disease could be attacking my body and just **show up** at a certain time, and she believed that was why I hadn't been able to find the answer until now.

She called Sir Charles Gairdner Hospital and arranged for me to go there immediately for more tests. I would need a bone marrow biopsy and a few days in hospital so that they could educate me on what the treatment plan was. I was still very angry, but there was also a part of me that felt relieved; I got an answer, and now I could tackle it. My mum drove me home so I could get a bag of clothes and supplies, and then we headed to the hospital.

I called Patrick to give him an update, and he reassured me that he would meet me as soon as he could get off. Patrick had been my partner in life and business for the last five years – I'm sure getting this phone call would have been a huge shock. Little did I know that when he woke up that morning, he had been **planning** to leave me. He'd had enough. He was also frustrated with my health and it was taking a toll on him, too. The day was not panning out how he thought.

It took a few hours before I was admitted, and by then my sister had come to support me. Patrick had arrived earlier. I was taken to a private room in the cancer ward. My mother, my sister, and Patrick sat with me while I went through the whole introduction to cancer. We were given heaps of information, and then they ordered many tests. I had a bone marrow test, blood samples taken, and numerous other medical inspections. I was exhausted, but remember feeling the security of being in a hospital, getting the best care I could to get on the road to **recovery**.

I was in hospital for three days waiting for the results of the tests. They'd given me referrals and booked haematologist specialists for me to see so that I could find out more information on what to do next. I packed my things, and even had a bag with all the connections and goodies in it for cancer patients, the take-home pack. I was really impressed by this; it was very orderly and organised.

Patrick and I walked into my first specialist appointment, and I was told that my only option to cure CML was a bone marrow transplant. I would need to find a blood match to make this possible. The doctor said that in his opinion I would have a 60% chance to live more than five years after the operation – meaning that 40% of people who have the transplant die within the five years. Bone marrow transplant is the strongest type of chemotherapy you can ever have. It wipes out your whole immune system on the chance that it will kick back in.

The transplant process takes about **four weeks**, and I would need to be completely isolated throughout that time in a private, special room and area of the hospital. This was daunting to me, even for one as optimistic as I am. My only other medical choice was to take a drug called Interferon, having daily injections of a drug that makes you feel as though you have a severe virus. That didn't seem like a very good quality of life. The doctors told me to put my life in order and that if there was something I wanted to do, to do it – basically, prepare to not live a long time. After a few weeks of talking to my family and digging deep into what I wanted to do and what **risks** I was going to take to survive this disease, I decided that my best option was the bone marrow transplant. I had to be positive about it and just hope for the best.

I went into bone marrow transplant preparation. I had to go through IVF because after having the transplant there would be no options for me to naturally conceive children. Specialists sent me to the IVF specialist, Dr Anne, who was the fertility queen in Perth at the time. I was so lucky that she was prepared to help me, and she offered me full financial cover knowing that this was my only option of having children, also given the fact that I actually had to survive the cancer first.

Having children always seemed very important to me, so I started IVF. This process requires you to inject yourself with special drugs over several weeks, preparing your eggs to be harvested in an operation. Retrieving my eggs was going to be a **one-chance** shot, and they had to get enough eggs as this would be my only opportunity to become a mother at some stage. Because they didn't store eggs at this time, my only option was to fertilise my eggs and have them frozen, to utilise them when I was ready. After discussing this with Patrick, he agreed that he was happy to be the father of my embryos.

The egg retrieval operation was done at Mount Hospital in Perth. It was over in a few hours, but when I got back to my ward I came down with ovarian hyperstimulation syndrome (OHSS). I was not well – basically, my body had started drowning in its own fluid. It's a very dangerous situation to be in, and it was causing quite a panic. My specialist doctor needed to put fluid drains inside me to relieve some of the pressure. A week after the operation I was still in hospital. I looked like I was fully pregnant because I had that much fluid in my abdominal area, putting pressure on all my organs.

I was sent to intensive care, because the situation became life-threatening. I spent four days there, absolutely frightened to death, and my body was out of control. I couldn't walk; I was basically lying on a bed like a big balloon. Breathing was difficult – *everything* was difficult. I couldn't go to the toilet by myself, too. I remember that I once had to ask Patrick if he could wipe my bottom after I went to the toilet. I actually felt more comfortable with him doing it, rather than a nurse, as I needed to do No. 2. It was one of those points in my life where I felt completely humiliated. I'm guessing that's what women feel like when they have a baby, and they have to let all their inhibitions go. Patrick did that day, I was so **thankful** and so touched. This was a very difficult thing to ask your partner to do.

Several times throughout the three weeks that I was in hospital, my mother, sister, and Patrick broke down in tears because they felt so hopeless, and they were scared and worried. This was heartbreaking to see, but I was just trying to survive. I was exhausted; I could have easily given up – if I had a button that I could press to take myself out of this life, I would have been tempted. It took nearly four weeks for my body to take back control of itself, but I recovered and I got on with my life. From the IVF experience, I retrieved many good eggs, and with Patrick's sperm we fertilised 11 healthy, strong embryos. It was a very surreal feeling.

I then worked on getting my blood levels in a more normal order, so I had to go on that drug Interferon after all. The first time I took it I thought I was going to die. The doctors explained to me that the first time is really quite horrific, but after that things should get slightly better. My entire body was screaming out and burning in pain. I could feel every nerve system in my body on fire. I tried to meditate and talk myself out of noticing this pain, but it was excruciating. To **describe it**, it feels like your body has had acid thrown on it. I woke up feeling completely exhausted, but totally relieved that I was still alive.

A light-hearted moment occurred – the morning after that experience, my mother had come over to spend time with me, and I was discussing how distraught I felt and how awful the night was. I was feeling very stressed. We were sitting in the lounge room having a cup of tea, and I looked down at my hands. They were turning blue. We both started to panic, so we called the doctor and explained to him that my hands had gone blue and I was really worried – it looked like they were dying. My doctor, Dr Steve Ward, said, 'Kristie, look, I assure you that having blue hands has got nothing to do with the side effects of Interferon. I don't know why your hands are blue – are you cold?'

I hung up still worried about my blue hands; it just didn't seem right, and we were highly sensitive to all the dramas of having leukaemia, but we just didn't know how and why my hands were blue. It dawned on us about half an hour later that my hands were blue because I was rubbing them on my legs – I was wearing a new pair of jeans and the dye was coming off. It was a funny moment in the midst of all the stress and anxiety. My mother and I just laughed and laughed, and we knew that we would look back on this story and just go, 'Oh, my God'. I should have washed the jeans before I wore them, but it was absolutely hilarious. Those blonde moments amongst all the **craziness** are things that keep you going, and make you realise that you've got to laugh.

The second injection of Interferon was nowhere near as crazy and painful, and after three months of putting up with this drug, I was thrown a lifeline on 20 June 2001 in the form of a trial drug called ST1571, later called Glivec. With this drug, I had almost immediate results. I was on the trial for three months, and my life had turned around. There was hope, light, excitement. **Every day** I felt like I could take one more step than I could the day before, with less pain and a lot more energy and vibrancy. Every breath I was taking at this point I was thanking God for this drug that was giving me the energy and the will to live.

But then the bad news came again, and I was told that the trial drug was stopping. The only way to access this drug that gave me my life back was to pay in excess of $50,000 per year. I wasn't a wealthy person; in fact, my business had suffered because of my illness, and I hadn't recovered financially. This news was another death sentence. Why was I given so much hope, only to have it ripped away?

It was clear to me that without this drug I would be back to preparing for a bone marrow transplant. The **success** that this drug had with other patients on the worldwide trial had generated a huge amount of media attention, and built up the hopes of all the CML sufferers here in Australia.

I had to personally place my life in the hands of the Australian Government by asking for their support in making Glivec affordable by placing it on the Pharmaceutical Benefits Scheme.

Plea to PM: Save my life

ONLY HOPE: Leukemia patient Kristie Dean is 30 but says she will die without a $55,000-a-year drug. Picture: JODY D'ARCY

By NADIA MIRAUDO

PERTH leukemia patient Kristie Dean has pleaded with the Prime Minister to save her life.

The 30 year old, who was diagnosed with Chronic Myeloid Leukemia (CML) 18 months ago, says she will die because the Federal Government has refused to subsidise a drug which costs more than $55,000 a year.

She has written to John Howard urging him to place the drug Glivec — known as the magic bullet — on the Pharmaceutical Benefits Scheme. Glivec targets cancer cells more effectively than other treatments and has fewer side effects.

If listed on the scheme, the breakthrough drug would cost as little as $23 a month. It would cost just $4 a month for pensioners.

Last month, the Pharmaceutical Benefits Advisory Committee announced it would not subsidise the drug for those suffering from the early stages of CML.

Only patients in the last stages of the disease will be subsidised. The news has shattered Ms Dean.

"I'm trying to remain calm, but it is very surreal," she said.

"To actually be told that it is not going to be subsidised is not a good enough answer when you are going to lose your life."

She said there was no way she could afford the drug without the subsidy.

When Ms Dean began using Glivec as part of a trial nine months ago, 97 per cent of her cells were being attacked by the disease. She is now in remission, with only 0.3 per cent of her cells affected.

"The Government spends millions of taxpayer dollars on research and when they come up with a drug that is the closest to a cure that we have, they make it inaccessible," she said. "If I don't get the drug I'll die. There is no nice way of saying it."

Leukaemia Foundation of WA chief executive officer Sheryl Grimwood said without Glivec, those in the early stages of CML would have less than two years to live.

A spokeswoman for the Pharmaceutical Benefits Scheme said the committee would reconsider the situation if another application was made.

The Fight of My Life

*'If the only prayer you ever say in your life is thank you, that would **suffice**.'*

– Meister Eckhart

Extracts from Kristie's letter

Dear Mr Howard,

On the 23rd October 2000, I was diagnosed with CML (Chronic Myeloid Leukemia).

I had bone-marrow biopsy, blood samples and numerous medical inspections and looked at having a bone-marrow transplant.

Luckily, my brother, Jay, was a 5-out-of-6 match. The transplant specialist said I would have a success rate of 60 per cent to live 5 years after the operation.

My only medical choice was to take a drug called Interferon…having to daily inject myself with a drug that made me feel as though I had a severe virus every day. I had no energy to live. I needed to be cared for continually by my mother and I was on pain-relief tablets every three hours.

After 3 months of putting up with this I was thrown a lifeline in the form of the Glivec trial on June 20, 2001.

With this drug I had almost immediate results. I have been on the trial now for over nine months and my life has indeed turned around.

There is hope, there is light, there is excitement. I have dreams to be a mother, a wife, to work in helping others less fortunate. Every breath I take I thank God for this drug that has given me energy again and the will to live.

Now I'm told that I'll have to pay in excess of $55,000 a year to have this drug. This news is another death sentence.

I am placing my life in your hands asking for your support in making this drug affordable by placing Glivec on the PBS list.

Regards,
Kristie Dean

The fight was on to save my life. I wrote to John Howard urging him to place Glivec, known as the 'Magic Bullet', on the Pharmaceutical Benefits Scheme (PBS). Glivec targets cancer cells more effectively than any other treatment, and with fewer side effects. If it was listed on the scheme, this **breakthrough** drug would cost as little as $23 per month, $4 for pensioners. The Pharmaceutical Benefits Advisory Committee (PBAC) announced it would not subsidise the drug for those suffering from the early stages of CML, and only patients in the last stages of the disease would be subsidised. The news shattered me. I was trying to remain calm, but it was very surreal. To just be told that it was not going to be subsidised was not good enough of an answer when you are going to lose your life.

When I first started using Glivec as part of a trial, 95% of my cells were being attacked by the disease, but after nine months I was in remission with only 0.3% of my cells affected. But I couldn't afford the treatments, not when they weren't subsidised. I can't tell you how that feels other than pure panic, stress, and complete anxiety, things that I didn't need to feel when fighting for my life. I just didn't understand; the government spends millions of tax dollars on research, and when they come up with a drug that is as close to the cure that we have, they make it inaccessible. If I didn't get the drug, I would die – there was no nice way of saying it. Even the Leukaemia Foundation of WA Chief Executive Officer Shirley Grimwood said that without Glivec in these early stages of CML, we'd have less than two years to live.

A spokeswoman for PBS said the committee would consider the situation if an appeal was made, so the **fight** was on. Royal

Perth Hospital consultant haematologist Richard Herrmann said, 'We hope Glivec would be replaced from Interferon as a treatment, because Interferon was debilitating for patients'. The facts were that in clinical trials of more than 9000 people around the world, 90% of the patients in early CML who had no longer responded to therapies were in remission after taking the drug. Glivec acts as a brake on the process of leukaemia by inhibiting an enzyme that makes white blood cells divide. The drug trademarked under the name of Glivec was hailed a landmark in the battle against the disease, because it targets cancer cells much more effectively than current drugs and has fewer side effects. All these facts were accumulating and there was nothing I could do but **take action** and get the plea on its way, because the $50,000 price tag was too much.

A few Glivec patients who were on the trial came together, and we called ourselves the Glivec Group. It was time for us all to pull together and use the power of the people to change these laws to save our lives. We had to action our voices to keep our cause in the face of the decision makers. We needed to have a **constant flow** of letters targeted to specific politicians to have the most impact. The Prime Minister and his wife were also on that list.

Time was critical. I would like to recognise Bill Sutton, Lynda Crane (and her husband, Keith Crane, for his support), Margaret Spry, Pam Flint (and her husband, Bill), Simon Pontiflex, Kristen Ridgeway, Mary Barrelt, Monique Hillman (and her husband Ivan Hillman), Bill Mackenzie and Jan Mackenzie, and my partner Patrick Pope for their dedication to the fight!

We were having meetings and phone calls after phone calls, helping each other, supporting each other, and getting petitions into the government. I personally wrote letters to Parliament House in Canberra, and directly to John Howard, the Pharmaceutical Benefits Branch, every department or government office we could think of. As you could imagine, the energy behind saving your own life is very powerful. My personal story appeared on *A Current Affair*, *Today Tonight*, Channel 9 News, and a news article in the *Sunday Times*.

I'll never forget the phone call I got one day in the middle of all this turmoil and terror. I was living in Scarborough, Perth at the time, and I was standing out in my backyard with Patrick and my mum, getting some fresh air in between us being on the phone and **writing letters** and constant talk about what we were going to do. I answered the phone and it was the Leukaemia Foundation. They had amazing news for me, and this was their message:

'Kristie, I would like to let you know that in the last **couple of days** we've had someone come into the Leukaemia Foundation and sign documents and paperwork so that they can pay for you to have Glivec. This person would like to stay anonymous, and they read your story in the *Sunday Times* and was very touched and wanted to help you. We've been working with them for a few days to make that possible for you, Kristie.'

This was one of the most powerful phone calls I've ever had in my life. Here I was, fighting for my life to get the drug to survive, and someone with an **amazing heart** read my story and had set themselves up to pay for my treatment. My heart was just full of love. I needed to sit back down on the chair, because everything around me felt so surreal. Even telling this story now I'm full of tears and gratitude and love, and it's actually very difficult for me to speak because of the emotion of that day. That phone call will touch my heart forever.

Someone offering to help save my life was just the most powerful moment that someone could ever have. I don't know to this day who that person was, but I often think about them and send them love and gratitude; they must be very special to have the power to do that. It's just incredible. I've always had my **suspicions** of who it could be just from daydreaming, but at the end of the day I hope this person might read this book and know that I want to say thank you, thank you so much for that offer. You truly changed my heart that day, feeling the most powerful giving of a stranger that anyone could have.

Hearing this news meant I was able to relax and breathe; I could feel the weight coming off my shoulders. I knew that we had to still fight for this drug, but I felt a bit of space – I was going to be okay. Finally, after months of meetings, letters, petitions, and media stories, we did it. The PBS announced that Glivec would be added into the system, and lives could be changed. This was **a powerful moment** for all patients; we now had a chance to get the drug affordably, and the opportunity now to just concentrate on our health and get on with our lives.

I feel so lucky and blessed to have been part of that power group and to pave the way for future patients. That drug truly saved my life. I continued to use Glivec for about five years, and then after digging deep in my own mind and listening to my intuition, I approached my haematologist, Paul Canal, to say that I wanted to stop taking the drug. There was no **information** as to what would happen if I went off Glivec. His medical advice was to stay on it, but I was so headstrong that it was the best thing for me. I was prepared to take the chance. I'm not suggesting that you should do this, this was purely just my choice.

I can say this – I'm one lucky girl. I've now remained off Glivec for more than 10 years, and I've completely stayed in remission. It was a huge risk to do this, considering there was no documentation in the world that would back this being a good decision. A lot of people would think that it was crazy. When I have been asked over the last few years what I've done to keep myself in remission, I give this advice – I was **determined** to keep positive, always. I never wanted to become my disease. I always believed that the power of the mind has astonishing power over the body. I got on with my life and I didn't think about my disease every single day. You have control over your mind, and that has **control** over your body!

I choose to be the boss of me.

Some words from people who have benefited from Glivec:

Sue Hurt: 'A ripple effect – many now have life because of your early advocacy.'

Helen Troy: 'Bless you, Kristie, your advocacy meant my partner was able to access Glivec.'

Judy Telford: 'I relapsed after a transplant in 2004. I had no idea Glivec existed. My doctor told me I was the third person he had written a script for. I would have to have been in a trial otherwise, and I would not have qualified. Thanks for all you did.'

Tracey Macdonald: 'Thanks, Kristie, for sharing your story. When I realised that I had been diagnosed with the same condition as you, I knew that there was hope. That treatment was available, largely successful, and on the PBS thanks to your efforts.'

Jennifer Bilkey: 'Thanks, Kristie, your story is amazing. Thank you for giving me and many others the opportunity to use Glivec. I, too, would not have been able to afford it if it wasn't for the PBS. I wish you well and look forward to your book.'

Stephanie Parry: 'A big thank you to you, Kristie Dean. I was diagnosed in 2005 and went straight onto Glivec, albeit in a trial. Thank you for all your hard work and advocacy to get it onto PBS. **Looking forward** to your book coming out.'

Brad Smith: 'Good on ya, Kristie. My journey is very similar to yours; being diagnosed in '98, still on Glivec but just take a few when I feel like it. I'm 000.01 each visit, sweet as, so thanks for your campaigning. My cheaper meds are a benefit not only to me but so many others.'

Life is not about how many times you fall

It's about what you do after you fall.

He who gets up time and time

Again, will never fail.

So just keep getting up.

International Mum

'The Divine Love is here. We need only **unclench** our fists and open to it.'

– Jeanette Berson

I put my sneakers on, my dog in the car, and headed down to the west coast highway of Perth for a 7km walk. It was 26 degrees, the ocean was absolutely beautiful, and my heart was feeling blessed with love – not only to live in this amazing city of Perth, but to look back and reflect on parts of my life. I took a deep breath and could **feel** the sun shining on my face. I looked down at this beautiful blue, clear water. The air was still. It was one of those moments when I think, 'Wow, life is just an amazing story – the way it unfolds and twists and teaches us, it's just truly a gift that we should never take for granted'.

After being diagnosed with leukaemia, working out my strategy for survival, getting my hands on the Glivec drug and seeing the results almost immediately, I now had to plan how I was going to spend my time healing without the stress of the future, allowing my body to have that time mentally. How could I get the most out of my life as my body reclaimed itself from the Philadelphia chromosome invasion, leukaemia? How could I heal the child abuse road map that I had etched inside of my neuropaths? I look at my life as the most **important job** that I'll ever have. Now that I had a drug that was helping my body, I could see a future, not an end. So, I asked myself, 'What's my next plan?'

My heart has a passion for knowing more about the world. I love being around positive people and making an impact on this world. I dream about the world, about travelling and learning about different cultures and understanding the whole world that we live in, as we are just one tiny little part of it here in Perth. I know that my body always felt calmer and at peace when I could see the ocean at sunset; the waves and the salt water have always been a major part of my life.

I moved into a beach house in City Beach. It's a huge old place, with amazing ocean views. There were six bedrooms and three bathrooms. This house was old, but **very unique**, with lots of different levels. Most importantly I had the ocean view, and the ocean air to help heal my mind and body. I then had to think about how I could incorporate all these things that I loved to do into my future, whilst still allowing my body to heal.

I decided that I wanted to share my home with international students who were coming to Australia to learn English. This would give me the opportunity to learn about **different cultures**, support and help them, all while helping share the costs of day-to-day living at home. This was a huge opportunity for me because I didn't have the money to travel the world, so I thought, 'Why don't I bring the world to me?' During the next decade, I opened my home to different international students from all around the world. Many were from Switzerland, some from Japan, and China, and a Mexican boy, Carlos. I had a lot of French students, also, and some Korean, German, and Taiwanese. I started learning things about the world that I'd never heard – Switzerland has lots of different languages, Swiss German, Swiss Italian, Swiss French, meaning that one country really can't **communicate** with each other without English.

I understood the power of the English language and how important it is in the world for growth and strength in so many countries. I had students from all over the world needing to come and learn English to better their lives so that they could read manuals, study better, and have more opportunities in their own countries. This is something that we take for granted in Australia, because we speak English already. I had the opportunity to fill my home up with laughter and **love and security**, and be able to support and help all of these kids from around the world. This was something I always missed having as a child; a safe, positive, encouraging, loving family. I've always been a mothering kind of person so this suited me down to the ground.

This arrangement was called homestay, offering a bedroom with clean sheets and meals throughout the week. I was responsible for washing their clothes, and making sure they were safe and okay. I was a bit of a tour guide for them in Perth, showing them how to get to school, and taught them some general rules in Australia. Most had very basic English skills, and some had very little English at all, so that made communicating very interesting; lots of hand signals and pictures and smiles and love. Body language was very important.

I was determined to give the best **family** home that I could to my international guests over the years. We'd often be sitting around talking about life, and we always ate dinner together. At dinner, they could share the experiences they'd had throughout the day, talk about their own country, and also get to practice English. It was a tradition in my home that when we set the table for dinner, we would use my affirmation cards. They were power words that would both teach them a new word, and also open up a conversation. Other cards would give them a little life skill guidance. These helped us get to know each other and form a bond so that their time in Australia was always a good memory.

I remember one dinnertime with a few of us, Carlos wasn't looking very well, kind of sad. 'Carlos, why are you so sad tonight? What is wrong? You look really worried,' I asked him. Carlos replied, a tremor in his voice. He said, 'I'm very sorry and just very worried about my cousin. She was kidnapped in Mexico and we're worried about her safety. We don't know if she will return to the family'. I was not expecting that to come out of his mouth. We take our safety in Australia for granted, but kidnapping was very common when you come from an **influential** family in Mexico; it's something that happens on a daily basis.

Some of the dinner conversations were so profound that it would change my way of thinking about the world. Carlos struggled with the public transport in Perth because he was very paranoid when people were friendly towards him and used eye contact when he was on the bus to and from school in the city. He would come home a bit frightened and share with me that he felt like someone was watching him in the bus. I needed to spend quite a bit of time with Carlos explaining that this was normal; Australians are very friendly and curious, eye contact is normal for us and talking to a stranger on a bus is just polite. He told me that this is completely unusual in his country and that it was dangerous to travel around. He always needed to be accompanied by others so there was power in numbers. His country, he explained, was very corrupt and **dangerous**, so you could never relax when you were just out in public.

I never forget one Taiwanese girl coming to me one day amazed that we had dark blue water in our toilets, unheard of in her country. I had no idea what she was talking about, and then realised that I had used a Blue Loo that makes the water come out of the system all blue. She thought this was normal for us, as you would if you didn't know. It was hilarious. Quite a few times at a certain time of the year a group of young Chinese boys would stay for a couple of weeks on a school tour from a private school in Hong Kong. All of these boys had rich fathers in Hong Kong, businessmen. They had no siblings, the only sons in their **families**. They were like little emperors; they were rich, and they had everything done for them, so spending a few weeks in Australia at the beach was very interesting.

They wouldn't dare use public transport, so they would have to get taxis everywhere – they had never been on public transport before, and they had the money. A few of these boys' budget just for spending money would be at least about $1000AUD per week. Their concept of life was completely different. I remember a few of them had even bought push bikes and lots of electronics, even though they were here just for a few weeks. One group in particular would sneak out after I'd gone to bed at night, and two of them had fake IDs so they hit the casino, even though they were only 15 and 16 years old. I had no idea that this was going on until the school contacted me **wondering why** the boys were sleeping on their desks all day. They were very naughty boys, and they were sent back to their country early. I'm guessing now that a lot of these boys are now becoming the future businessmen of the world.

I learnt a lot about different cultural behaviours and habits; many countries do different things in the bathroom, like Koreans have a habit of splashing water around when they're cleaning up. I also got to experience a lot of different menus, as my guests were very keen to share their traditional food. We would do lots of cooking classes and experiment with different types of food.

I had a little Maltese Shih Tzu named Sammy, and he was my best friend. He was healing for the students when they'd come to stay, because when they were scared and not sure about what their future would be here in Australia, as well as having the pressure of studying and learning English, Sammy was right there, cuddling up with them. Dogs can sense someone's feelings, so he was an amazing Australian host. Sammy became quite famous internationally. He had photos with people from all around the world. They took him on walks, and I remember one French boy walking back from the **beach** carrying Sammy because Sammy just wouldn't walk any more – he'd put the skids on. European boys loved walking Sammy because it was a way to talk to people; the dog would attract not only the girls, but lots of Australians wanting to say hello. I used to joke and say that I should **hire him** out to people.

One afternoon one of the Swiss French boys, Florian, came home really upset. He only had about a month left of his nine month stay in Australia, and he didn't pass his medical test that would allow him to do a diving course here. It was his dream to do it, and it was a lot cheaper than back home. I could see his heart was broken, and he was very frustrated and quite angry. We sat down near the pool and I said, 'Florian, maybe there's a reason why you are not passing this **balance** test. What if something goes wrong? What if it's just not meant to be? What if life is protecting you from the fact that this is just not the right time to do this?' Florian was only 17 years old and this logical explanation wasn't something that he wanted to hear, but I continued being positive and said, 'Look, I'm sure that there's a bigger reason why you shouldn't be doing this dive course. Just hang in there, mate, you've had a great time in Australia. It's just not meant to be this time'.

Florian left Australia just a few weeks after that conversation, and within a couple of weeks of being back in Switzerland he was diagnosed with an air bubble in his spine. If he had pushed the results, or gone to another doctor to get the medical clearance, he could have died. Unbeknownst to me, that conversation I had with him could have saved his life. It was a **huge lesson** that he still remembers. Florian and I have remained friends for nearly a decade now, and I consider him to be one of my international children. He refers to me as his Australian mum. He's now enjoying his life; he's married and has a beautiful baby girl. He has visited me in Australia many times over the years and we have felt nothing but love and a strong bond that is truly like nothing else.

There were quite a few guests who stood out to me over the years. I **fell in love** with two Japanese girls who lived with me for more than three years. Natsuki was only 15 when she first arrived, and she went through high school here. She was an amazing and beautiful girl, very personable. She loved her music at Churchlands High School so we were always going to concerts. She was involved in the community with all her friends. I remember we planned her dress for her school formal together. I was really like a mother to her in Australia, and seeing this little girl grow into a woman completely blew me away. I had no idea that this love would be so strong.

Yoh, who I now refer to as my **daughter**, came to Australia when she was about 19. She studied English for a year, and then got her childcare diploma. Wow – the bond, the love, the support, the holidays, the time we've had together has truly changed my life. I feel like God blessed me with the chance to experience how it feels to be a mother and have teenage girls, being able to support and give them advice and love. Yoh has returned to Australia after leaving for seven years, and has now been living here for many years. I'm very proud to say that they are two beautiful, **strong women**, and I know that through my help and guidance I had a huge part in making them who they are today. I created my own happy family memories, and I know that it healed a lot of my past. It gave me an opportunity to experience what it feels like to have a positive, loving family that I always craved.

Words from My International Family

a collection of stories

'I first got to beautiful Australia in 2006, **leaving** my lost paradise Reunion Island. I was almost 16, young and fresh. I entered a homestay with a local family. I can't remember their names, but the guy was really big, and the lady really old. What a shock for the little kid I was, in a foreign country where I could not even speak English – I spent two terrible, awkward months with them. They were too old to adapt to the young, super active, and ambitious boy I was. I wanted to conquer Perth, but had to stay home. I was introduced to a little Reunion Island community and met people who were my age. One of the girls, "Lou" was telling me about her super cool homestay with Kristie, this super cool mama. Lou was leaving Australia and knew about the uncomfortable situation I was in at my homestay, so she gave me the opportunity to meet Kristie. She had told me so much about that big house in City Beach, living the Australian **dream**. Kristie and I understood each other immediately; she already knew who I was, and I could feel her strong personality, as well. The house

I Am Now

*hosted a few students from all around the world, facing the beach, my Australian dream would start **really soon**.*

*Kristie offered me the room that was most suited to me, the one you could access straight from the garden, and the garage (haha)! She had that capability to understand people and give trust, but you should not mess around with her or she could get mad. She had a lot of responsibilities with underage students. Kristie was always here for us; she loved having dinner with all of us, and always made me feel comfortable. She was my OZ mama and knew that it wasn't easy for us to be away from our home. I remember our lunch box always ready in the freezer for us to eat, and barbecues at sunset. Kristie looked after that big house and students by herself. She gave me the freedom to do whatever I wanted with her two eyes open to what I was doing without entering my **private life**; she always had the balance, and the right advice. The good thing with Kristie was definitely her straightforwardness – if something was wrong you would know it, but she wasn't spiteful. Kristie was part of my emancipation. She took good care of me and of all the others who stayed with her. What an amazing time we had. I would leave my own children with her for them to live the same as I did ... Thank you, Mama.'*

    Romain Dufourg, Reunion Island

'I was a 16 year old student, freshly arrived in Australia from Reunion Island when I moved in with Kristie. Kristie was living in a house facing the sea. She was already hosting other students when I arrived. They quickly became big brothers and **sisters** to me because I was the youngest in the house. Despite Kristie's disease that made her suffer a lot, she was always strong for all of us and never stopped smiling. She was a role model, and she made me want to be as strong and open-minded as her. She helped me find myself in Australia and inspired me to **discover the world**. I will never thank her enough for that. She will always be a mother to me, and I hope that life will offer her everything she deserves. I love you, Kristie. Kisses from somewhere in the world.'

    Lauryane Arnassan, Belgium

'I arrived in Perth in 2004 to study English and childcare when I was 18. During that time Kristie was my host mother for three years. I went back to Japan to become a children's English teacher, and I came back to Perth to live with Kristie in 2013. I can hardly believe that 13 years has gone by this quickly. Kristie has been my lovely OZ mother for the duration of this amazing experience. I truly felt welcomed as part of her family.

Thank you so much for helping me to **immerse myself** in my everyday life in Australia. These special moments were amazing. What is more, you gave me lots of personal opportunities to become a strong woman. While staying with you, my favourite thing was living with people from overseas. We had lots of fun together; the trip down south, visiting your grandmothers, horse races, we did so much! It has been such a blessing staying with you. You have made this such an **educational**, memorable, and amazing experiences, and I am always thinking fondly of the time we were able to spend together. I can't express how much I appreciated you opening your arms to me. Being a part of your life was a unique experience for me, especially because it was a totally exciting time. I´ve learnt a lot and I am simply thankful for all different experiences I´ve gathered. They made me who I am now.'

    Yoh Araki, Japan

'I was 15 when I first arrived in Perth. I was introduced to Kristie as my guardian. Through my three years at high school, Kristie took care of me and introduced me to a whole new culture: BBQs, horse races, trips down south and my 16th, 17th, and 18th birthdays. Being my Aussie mother and sometimes friend must have been very hard to balance for you, when I think back. We got into lots of arguments. I hated you so many times, and loved you for so many more moments. But sure, we built this beautiful and **amazing bond** between us. My experience in Perth definitely brought me up as a strong woman and I'm glad I became the way I am now. All the tears and laughter we shared are truly my precious memories.'

Natsuki Asada, Japan

'I came to Australia in September 2003 at the age of 19, and I felt healthy. After a few months, I wanted to get my PADI diving license. I had to pass a medical test at the Perth Medical Centre and the doctor said no, as he saw that I had no balance, and for him it meant neurological issues. Well, stubborn and stupid as I was, and because I had already dived six metres in Greece, I called my doctor in Switzerland to write a letter for me saying that I was healthy. The Aussie doctor said he wasn't really feeling completely safe about it, but approved it.

I had to stop during my **first lesson** because I wasn't good enough at swimming. I was disappointed, but I had other options to enjoy Australia, which I did thanks to Kristie. She helped me understand it wasn't the end of the world to not do this diving course, some things are just not meant to be.

I went back home and my symptoms got worse and worse. Diplopia, horrible pain in my head when sneezing (had to lie down when it happened), motor issue (legs), and inverse temperature feeling on my legs. I went to my uncle (a doctor) who sent me to a neurologist and after a scan he found out that I had an Arnold Chiari Malformation.

After surgery I felt good, even if I still have motor issues, especially with my legs. But at least I wasn't quadriplegic, as I could have become. **Today**, I still have myotonia as a consequence of my sickness, but I feel good and am blessed to be married to the perfect woman and have a beautiful daughter.'
    Florian Chardonnens, Switzerland

'It is hard to describe in just a few words the wonderful time that I spent in Western Australia back in 2004. Kristie undoubtedly played a huge part in it. I could call her a substitute mother, which is already quite an expression, but frankly speaking Kristie was even more than that. Young and generous in her heart, Kristie became very quickly a benevolent friend, with plenty of love and fun to give. Things **immediately** clicked between us and I knew that the bond created was going to be everlasting. Nowadays, whenever I reminisce about those days in City Beach, my heart aches with nostalgia. Hopefully one day I can meet her again and feel that fantastic vibe emanating from that lovely lady!'
    Darius Rao, Geneva-Switzerland

New York, Amazon Jungle

'Ayahuasca, known as the Spiritual Mother of all Plants. **Medicines** in the Amazon Rainforest. She will call you.'

– Kristie Dean

Perth, Dubai, New York, Peru, Lima, Iquitos, and then into the Amazon Jungle – it was February 2012 and, man, was I excited. This was the solo trip of my life. I packed two suitcases, one for New York, and one for Peru as I'd be going from one extreme climate to another; the fast pace of New York, the Big Apple, then into Peru, South America, and after that into the Amazon jungle.

48 hours until take-off, and the city of New York was calling my name. So was Ayahuasca, the mother of all medicines in the Amazon rainforest. It's said that the spirit of the Ayahuasca plant medicine will call out to your spirit. The Ayahuasca medicine is said to teach us our strengths and weaknesses, stripping away the psychosomatic blockages, and restoring our natural health and perception. It penetrates our nervous system and renews conduits of energy, deliberated by toxins, stress, confusion, and anxiety. Ayahuasca inspires with spiritual visions and wisdom to **manifest** positive changes in personal lives, and guides us through the huge quantum leaps in the evolution as human beings. This calling is a powerful one.

In the hours before I was to start the journey of my life, my subconscious mind started fighting the experience and I had breathing difficulties, pains in my tummy, and I was sweaty and dizzy. I was panicking because I had to get on a **plane and fly** across to the other side of the world. There was no way I could fly feeling this ill. The best thing to do was to visit a doctor, at least to get a medical certificate because if I couldn't fly I needed my health insurance to protect me. The doctor said I was too unwell to fly, so I headed home to rest. I was overwhelmed with sadness and disappointment.

12 hours before the first flight, I was sitting on the lounge and had an epiphany. I believe what was happening to me was stress and anxiety from the plant medicine calling me; it was testing me, trying to stop me. I knew that I had to meditate and talk to the part of myself that was frightened and not allowing me to go. I took a **deep breath** and told myself, 'Kristie, you can do this. You are meant to experience the Ayahuasca. This is an experience of a lifetime, and your body is just tricking you with fear and anxiety. Release and let go. Release and let go. Trust and love. Trust and love'.

I came out of this **meditation** with new eyes and felt completely at peace. There had been a shift. Miraculously, I felt okay – I could breathe easier, I felt relaxed, and didn't feel like vomiting. I wasn't dizzy, and I didn't have a temperature. From that second, I didn't look back. I was going to experience Peru and New York, and nothing was stopping me. I flew ten hours straight to Dubai for a stop, and then on to New York. The New York flight was another 14 hours from Dubai.

My New York homestay family was picking me up from the airport. I had researched them and booked online, so we'd never met before. Homestay is an amazing way to travel because it's very cheap. It cost me just over $240 per week for all my accommodation, breakfast, and dinner. I was only in New York for a couple of nights and then I would fly to Peru, so I could leave one suitcase in New York and return for it on the way back home. The family picked me up in their 4WD and welcomed me into their large home in Ridgewood. I'd never seen snow in my life, and it started lightly snowing. I was so damn excited, I could've done **a happy dance** in the street.

I had 48 hours in NY to balance out the time difference and jet lag from travelling. I spent a little time walking around my new neighbourhood. It was amazing; it's an Old Dutch colony area, with all the history of the Dutch-style houses – very *Sex in the City*. My bedroom was very comfortable, and I had a view looking into the street. I couldn't believe I was there. I'd been to New York before but only as a tourist, and it was a dream to come back and feel what it was like to live in this massive city. What a contrast it would be; New York, and then the isolation of then being deep in the Amazon. I didn't want to be a tourist this time; I just wanted to go where my legs took me, and watch the world go by, **contemplating life** and feeling alive.

I took two flights to get to the Amazon. The first one got me into the capital, Lima, and a smaller plane took me to the smaller city of Iquitos, in the top north of Peru. The only way to access Iquitos is to fly or **go by boat**, there's no road. It's very isolated. I landed in Iquitos with my eyes wide open. I couldn't believe that I could see an airplane wreckage on one side of the runway. It had been there for years, I suspect, but it wasn't something I wanted to see as we were landing.

I took a little bemo horse and cart to my accommodation where I stayed for a couple of nights before heading into the Refugio Altiplano retreat. The retreat is located roughly 30 miles outside Iquitos. Refugio Altiplano is on about 12,000 acres of Amazon jungle. I arrived there in the afternoon on a small boat, and met three others on the same journey from America. One couple was from California, and the other lady was from San Francisco. They had been to the retreat before, and were very excited for the ceremony that would happen tonight after our arrival. There was something so **magical** about the Amazon jungle. You could hear all the birds and wildlife; the jungle comes alive. The air I breathed felt cleaner, with no pollution; I was miles away from any city. I felt like I'd left the world behind.

I was taken to my own house in the jungle retreat, a huge two storey home with three balconies around it all to myself, all made from the local timber trees and flyscreen shade cloth. I settled my things and then headed up to the main house about 800m away for a bit of late lunch. Afterwards, I relaxed and reflected in my house, and prepared for the ceremony. I was going to get picked up by one of the retreat guards, so when it was dark outside I got ready. I made sure I put comfortable clothes on, and I got my big gumboots ready – you've got to wear your big rubber gum boots to protect you in the terrain. I gathered up some special blankets and sarongs that I was going to lay in the ceremony house. I'd also taken a handful of special **crystals** that I'd collected over the years from different places I had been. They had my energy embedded in them, so it was something physical and meaningful for me to take to ceremony.

The security guard picked me up. He was wearing a gun for protection, especially at night in the Amazon, and walked me over to the big ceremony house, a big, wooden hut with open sides that was covered by flyscreens to keep the insects out. There was around 15 of us there, and there were mattresses laid out, a bit like **camping out**. You could also gather yourself a plastic bucket that you'd maybe need if you were purging from taking Ayahuasca. I set my little blankets out, waiting for the ceremony to start. The lead shaman and two others sat up at the front at a table overlooking us.

We sat in the dim candlelight, and it was all **very quiet**; you could soak in the sensitivity of the jungle all around you. You couldn't help but feel more connected to the earth. The first 20 minutes was about getting yourself comfortable as the shamans prepared in the quiet. The shaman prepared the Ayahuasca into small cups, and each of us went up one after the other to take our medicine. As they called us up, the shaman had a personal chat with each of us for a few moments, setting the intent for our experience. The Ayahuasca is a foul-smelling brown liquid, so it's not very palatable – you need a little water to wash it down.

There was a wide bathroom area, six toilets with no walls between them. It's so everyone can use the toilet whenever they want, and no one is left alone unsupervised. There was a big emphasis on being looked after when you took the Ayahuasca. After my turn, I sat back down on my mattress and we had quiet time, and listened to the other shamans sing. After about one hour, I was not having any effects of the Ayahuasca. I was a bit disappointed; I'd come from the other side of the world to experience this **medicine** and this spiritual experience. I decided to tap the shaman on the shoulder and ask what he suggested I do. The American shaman said, 'Well, Kristie, we can't have that,' and poured me another cup.

I downed the juice, being a little bit cocky, and walked quietly back to my mattress. After only just a couple of minutes, boom – I was definitely feeling the effects. I felt like waves of energy were pounding rapidly throughout my body, almost making me dizzy and confused. Holy shit, how intense was this feeling? I could hear people around me now, belching and coughing, vomiting in the buckets. The shamanic **singing** was taking my brain outside of itself, feeling the energy of the song, the Ayahuasca sinking itself in every cell of my body and brain. Closing my eyes, I could feel waves of colour and energy like a kaleidoscope. I started to panic, feeling the need to take control of my mind, as I wasn't really enjoying it. Fear was overwhelming me. People were occasionally wandering over to the toilet and emptying themselves. I actually felt like vomiting quite a few times throughout the night, but couldn't seem to purge very well.

I guess you could call this a kind of living hell. Many people take Ayahuasca because they want to **clean their mind**. It's said that an Ayahuasca ceremony can equal hundreds of hours of psychotherapy. I wasn't there for that. For me it was about cleansing my body and my mind after cancer, and rebooting my neurosystem. I could feel the serotonin levels in my body rising, so I could actually feel a lot of love. Many other participants had visions and life lessons. For me, that never happened. My mind was so worried about dying that I didn't allow these lessons and visions to come in – well, that's what I believe.

The ceremony went for 4-5 hours. I can remember shamans coming up and blowing smoke on me, **touching** my body in different areas, using their healing hands. You needed to be looked after; it was like they needed to keep you alive. It was very scary. Then the ceremony was over, finished with light singing. More candles were lit and everyone slowly woke. I found it very difficult to come back whilst everyone was packing up and talking about their experiences, then making their way back to the house with the guard and his gun.

I was laughing a lot, and I found it very difficult to keep my balance. I was very dizzy. I was escorted back to my house with two security guards holding me up, walking me upstairs and putting me **to bed.** They made sure I had a bucket and water, and then they left. I remember laying there wondering if I was going to live through the night. I was so drugged, and had so many thoughts about my life. Different experiences from my life were replaying themselves. It was like my mind would not actually allow me to go to sleep.

The next day seemed to come very quickly, and I'm not sure whether I actually slept or was in a dream state, because I was completely conscious of what was happening. I had a cold shower, as there was no hot water in the jungle. The next few hours were spent quietly in the home by myself, spending a lot of time in the toilet, cleaning out. I didn't really know I had so much inside me – my toilet was my friend that morning. I could feel the serotonin levels still very high in my head, feeling so much love about everything that I could see. I was in a complete loving state of being, **blissing out**. During the next ten days in the jungle, I went to a ceremony every second day to experience more of the Jungle Juice. I took part in seven ceremonies all up.

During the day, I would go and do a few different things. There was a botanical garden in the estate where you could go and learn about different varieties of medicinal plants and herbs and how they would help heal illnesses of the body, and find out about their importance within the culture. This was very fascinating and, of course, the jungle was just so extraordinarily beautiful, so I soaked it up with everything I had.

After three weeks in Peru, it was time to further **experience life** in New York.

New York, New York, and I

I had no real plans, but to take each day as it comes, dreaming and feeling the air.

I travelled most days into Manhattan enjoying the subway culture,

*I loved to sit in the parks and **observe**, Central Park and Bryant Park were my favourites.*

I couldn't tell you how many times I ended the day at Times Square on my way home.

I love the power of solo travelling, it's definitely become a passion of mine.

I enjoy walking the earth, in the here and now, makes me feel truly alive.

I enjoy holidaying with me ...

Flashes of Life

'To the little souls who journeyed with me, I love you **unconditionally**. I bless you on your journey. I will see you again. Fly, fly, fly.'

– Kristie Dean

As you know, I had embryos frozen in preparation for a bone marrow transplant. I was hugely lucky never to have to experience that, as the odds of survival were very low. My journey took me through IVF, and I managed to freeze 11 high-quality embryos – our flashes of life. It was always a **great security** for me having those, as I didn't know what my future fertility options were going to be if I was going to stay on Glivec or other medications.

Fast-forward 10 years and my embryos were still frozen, and what an amazing journey that was; signing contracts, paying yearly for them to be frozen, and always wondering what my options were for them. I had been out of that relationship with my partner for 7-8 years by this point, but it was something that always kept us in contact with each other because we were legally bound by the embryos: they were 50% mine and 50% his.

I called Fertility North to **pay the account** and discuss some options, and was told there was a donor program finally being put in place. I was very excited about this as I just wanted the embryos to have a chance at life, because I'd nearly lost my own getting them. I went through this for a reason, and I wanted my embryos to come to life; if not with me, then somebody else who deserved the opportunity. I contacted my partner to tell him the situation and that it was very possible that we would have a chance to meet the offspring we created so many years ago.

Patrick is an amazing person, and having this history together felt more right than wrong. He was very open to looking at the donor process. He understood what I'd gone through to get them and how passionate I was about my embryos over the years. We both agreed that this was an amazing thing to do, so the process started. Appointments started at the fertility clinic, a group who make **dreams come true** for a lot of people. Everything just seemed to synchronise, like the whole process was meant to be. We never had any roadblocks setting this up. It also built a bit of excitement and amusement for the fertility doctors, because this was a new program for them. My partner didn't live in Perth so we had to do a psychological interview as part of the process, just to make sure that this was all legal and everything was agreed upon. We were put on a list. We had a bit of our history taken, and we basically had to sit in a file for couples to look at and **decide** whether they would like to choose us as donors.

We basically signed off our embryos and left them in the hands of the fertility clinic to make the right decisions. We knew that there was a place we could register our details so that the baby born from those embryos had a right to get a certain amount of **information** about us. We were very comfortable with this, and even considered being open donors. I guess that's just me; I like to be completely open with life and just let it flow.

A few years after this, I'd just come back from Peru and met up with Patrick. This was the first time we'd seen each other in nearly a decade, and we spent a bit of time talking about the medicines we were taking, our life journeys. We were just friends, completely friends; there was no **sexual attraction** between us, just pure respect and love for the part of our life that we'd shared. Being reunited 10 years later was an amazing blessing for me, seeing someone who meant so much to me. Both of us left letting things rest and heal from our past.

Flashes of Life

A few weeks after coming back from that trip, I was sitting in my lounge room wondering if a child had been born yet. I called the fertility clinic to touch base with them, and to ask if they had been donated to a family. Amazingly enough, I spoke to the coordinator of the embryo program and she said, 'Kristie, I've been trying to contact you!' I was totally surprised – why would she be contacting me? I explained to her that I'd been overseas, and I'd even reunited with the father of my embryos and we were wondering if any had been used.

She was **very surprised** about my journey, and she said, 'Kristie, I've been trying to contact you because no, we haven't used your embryos in a donor program yet, but we have two recipients looking at it and we'd like to know if you'd be open to donating them to two separate families. Because you've got a lot of embryos, this could be a good possibility'.

I said, 'Okay, so you mean we split them? Six here with one family and five with another family?' I was excited about this because I knew that would mean that it was an opportunity to make dreams come true for two families. I had always imagined one day being able to meet my genetic offspring. The fertility coordinator gave me a bit more information, without disclosing names of the two families, so that I could make a comfortable and **clear decision**, and then also pass this information on to my embryo daddy. After getting off the phone, I only contemplated it for about three minutes before I was straight on the phone to my mum, and then as quickly as possible called Patrick to get his opinion.

I probably had about 5-6 phone calls with the clinic and Patrick to find out what he thought, and came to the conclusion that I was **happy to** split the embryos and give the two families an opportunity. I then left that decision in the hands of the coordinator, and didn't hear much back for about two weeks. I never took any of these decisions lightly; I always felt a very spiritual connection to the embryos and the huge responsibility as a mum to do the right thing by them, guiding them. This felt completely right.

I was going around the house, doing the washing, moving the dog outside so that he could get some fresh air, and the phone rang. 'Hi, Kristie, this is the fertility clinic. Just letting you know that unfortunately we've come to the decision within the committee that we're going to take your embryos out of the donor program. I know you're not going to be happy with this decision, but you've got to understand on a legal point of view, in our **conversations** over the last few months you've said that you have had contact with the father of your embryos, and we are concerned if you two were ever to get back together again that you could get regret that you've put the embryos in the donor program'.

I could feel myself getting furious, my blood **pressure rising**, and I was short of breath because I had a major, physical panic. I was so excited about these embryos being in the program and having a chance at life, and now suddenly they had completely taken that away from me. I had no choice in the matter, and it was based completely on their presumption. I explained to her that it was never going to be, and how important it was for Patrick and I to have these embryos in the donor program; they had been frozen for more than 10 years and we wanted something done with them. I did not want them to think that I had gone through this process for nothing. But it didn't matter what I said; legally, we'd come to a grey area. 'Final decision,' she said. 'That's it, we're sorry, but we definitely have to take the embryos out of the program, and they'll be placed back into your care'.

When I got off the phone, I screamed and jumped up and down. I had to find myself again to accept that that phone call even just happened. Within seconds, of course, I was on the phone to my mum. She understood how desperate and frustrated I was. I called Patrick. There was a lot of swearing going on, and Patrick said, 'Kristie, trust that this is meant to happen and let's go one step at a time. You know that you believe in what's meant to be and obviously, this isn't what's supposed to happen'.

I remember this news taking quite a bit out of me. I dug deep and asked why this was **happening**. What did it mean? What were my options? I did not want the embryos to have been a waste of time, and I nearly died to get them. I knew that there must have been a bigger picture to the whole story, and I felt in my heart that there was. This brought up many conversations with my family to discuss what had happened. I'm very close with my brothers and mother, and we had gatherings and ask what they thought, and what my options were. I never thought that I would **contemplate** using the embryos myself, but was that why this happened? Were they choosing me to be their mum? What was I going to do?

Hmm. Big, deep decisions. I was not in a **relationship** with anyone, so I would be a single mum. Lots of my girlfriends would have thought that if anyone was going to have a bunch of kids, it would be me; I'm so motherly and maternal. It would be an exciting experience being a mother, but I always believed that it would happen if it was meant to, and here I was, faced with the possibility. After speaking with Patrick, he gave me permission to use the embryos. We discussed at length what that would mean legally, and how it would work. We both felt in our hearts that this was how it was meant to be. Patrick said, 'Kristie, I'll give you my full backing legally. I'll **sign the paper** for you to make this happen'.

I contacted Fertility North and explained that I was prepared to speak to the doctor about going through the process to become pregnant. I had an appointment with Dr Jay. It was quite a bizarre appointment because we had to move my details on the computer from out of the donor program into a completely different system, and this was unusual for them so it took a while to make sure everything was legally covered. Then the process would begin with me taking blood tests and starting the journey of IVF. In the first month, I had **blood tests** nearly every couple of days so they could work out my cycle, and I had internal tests to see how healthy I was and what my chances were for carrying a child. This all took a few months but, again, it just flowed. It was all very positive and looked good. I knew the odds and a decision was made that we would put two embryos in one transfer and see how they went.

Transfer day gave me a very weird, kind of strange feeling. I went to the fertility clinic and basically within a few seconds they'd inserted the embryos, and I could see on the ultrasound where they were placed. It was a wow moment, because there they were – I could literally see them sitting there inside myself, and then they were left to grow and adapt. I was monitored with blood tests over the next few weeks to see if I was going to become pregnant. It was weird waiting to know whether you're going to be a mum or not; exciting, but it also very surreal. But I was just going to be open and receptive. I didn't want to look back at this as an opportunity that was offered and regret not taking it.

This **transfer** didn't work, and I didn't become pregnant, so it was on to Phase 2. I went through the preparation with blood tests and monitoring, and getting my body ready for another transfer. It literally felt like a full-time job. If I wasn't at the clinic every second day, I was on the phone with them, or looking at different drug options to give me the best shot. I was on steroid tablets, oestrogen … it was full on. The second transfer day was a little different to the first because I knew what to expect. I was excited because my odds of getting pregnant were going up, looking at the numbers. I had put in so much effort to get to this point, with medications and doctor appointments. But, again, I didn't become pregnant.

I was still hopeful; I still had five embryos left, as I'd lost a few in the defrost stage. Getting ready for the third transfer, I was exhausted; it's a huge emotional ride. Your whole life completely revolves around making this little flash of life a reality. The third transfer was a really cool day. I invited my mum so she could experience what I was going through and so she could watch the embryos be planted into my uterus. This is kind of amazing; these little flashes have the opportunity to take this ride with you or not, and you can **feel the energy** strong in the air. The doctors and the nurses can feel the excitement, too, because it's a profound moment that literally can change your future.

I had mentally prepared myself to be strong, because it wasn't happening straight out. I prayed to God and said, 'Don't give me a path that's not good for me, please. I've gone through enough in my life, and I only want to feel enrichment. Please don't offer me this opportunity if it's going to be a hardship physically and mentally, because I understand that having a child is one of the most important, powerful things you can ever do in your life'. I knew that it was like two paths; it was either going to be a good path for my wellbeing and the future child, or it wasn't. I just knew that it needed to be set in a very strong, solid ground.

Mum and I went and had a **cup of tea** afterwards. It was funny, because I felt that after you have a transfer you kind of want to walk around slowly, not move around too much. You feel like you're holding a little egg inside you that you don't want to disturb. I remember feeling that when I needed to go to the toilet, I hoped that I wasn't peeing out my baby. You're just very sensitive to the fact that you've transferred a little future flash of life inside you.

It had been a few days, and it was time to follow up with blood tests to see if my levels had changed. I had mine before 7:00am, and sat in a waiting room with about 30 other women. After that, you go home, and it's a waiting game. The results don't come back until about 2:00 or 3:00 in the afternoon, and there were those 30 other women also ringing up to get their results. Some were just wanting to get results on what their blood levels were for that day, but some were waiting to know if they were pregnant or not.

I got a phone call. 'Kristie, I'm just informing you that unfortunately there's **no indication** that you're pregnant. I'm sad to say that it looks like it's not happened.'

'Okay,' I said, 'no problem. I was mentally prepared for that, thank you very much.' They insisted that I come in the next day and get another blood test to check everything was okay.

A few hours passed, and I got another phone call. 'Kristie, I'm really sorry about this, but we rang you with results that were not your results. I'm very sorry about this, we can't believe that this has actually happened. I can't explain it, other than it's our fault, and we want to let you know you are actually pregnant'.

I was in **complete disbelief**; a couple of hours ago I didn't think I was pregnant. I was having a bit of an out-of-body experience, because I wasn't sure I believed them. There had been a mistake, and they'd given me the wrong person's blood results. But I absorbed the information and screamed, 'Oh, my God, this is just crazy. It's actually happened. All this work and I'm pregnant'. I was meant to be a mum, and now my life was about to completely change. I repeated the blood test in a couple of days to make sure that I was actually pregnant and they confirmed it. I was definitely pregnant –

everything was going to plan, the blood levels were rising as normal. They told me to keep doing what I needed to do, but they had to continue monitoring me because it was still early days.

After a week and a half, devastating news. 'Kristie, I'm really sorry to give you this bad news, but the pregnancy has not held out. Your hormone levels are not rising as they should be, so unfortunately it's not going to be a healthy, viable pregnancy'.

So the emotional ride continued; my heart was devastated again, but my strength was still there. I'd done every single thing possible to make it happen and not let anything get in the way. I'd given it the best shot that I could ever give. I **continued** to be monitored because it was expected that I should get a period and that the miscarriage would happen naturally. However, my pregnancy hormones dropped, went still, and after a few more days rose back up again. This was very confusing for the doctors and the nurses. They couldn't explain it other than the fact that we did put two embryos in, and perhaps I may have had an ectopic pregnancy.

My hormone levels continued growing, but not at the speed that was normal. This was very stressful because it felt like one minute I was pregnant, then I wasn't. This went on for a few weeks, and I hadn't naturally had a period but the pregnancy hormone was still rising, though nowhere near what a healthy, normal pregnancy should be. Doctors started getting concerned, so they suggested I go to the emergency department at the hospital to get them to look into it further. There, I could at least plan to have a D&C if there was an ectopic pregnancy – with another baby growing somewhere, this could be a life-threatening situation. The decision was finally made that I must get the embryo removed via D&C.

It was really horrible, almost like a very premenstrual period; lots of cramping, stomach pain, and I was on pain relief tablets for about three days. I stayed in bed for much of the recovery time. It **was nothing** you'd want anyone to go through. About a month after this procedure had taken place I was sitting on the couch at home, and I suddenly had this very strong intuition that something was not right. I felt that the embryo was still inside me; I could feel a slight niggle in my abdomen. This feeling brought me instantly to the doctor and on the same day I was on a hospital bed. I was confused because I'd had a D&C, so what could it be? Lying there getting a very uncomfortable internal ultrasound, the nurses became shocked and repeated to me my history. Yes, I had just had a D&C four weeks ago, and there should not be any embryos inside of me. It was almost impossible, but there it was – a little embryo, dug deep into my uterus, clear as anything on the ultrasound.

The nurses couldn't believe it. They called in a doctor to check it again, and sent me immediately to call the fertility clinic. The embryo was still inside of me, not active, but it hadn't let go. This call caused alarm, because they'd never heard of this situation, but my **intuition** was completely right. I was upset because of the pain of having to go through the operation again, but I had to **surrender** to the situation because otherwise I could end up with an infection, and I just wanted to get healthy. I prepared for the second operation.

Changing the Scales

*'Sometimes surrender means giving
up to understanding
And becoming comfortable with not knowing'*

– Eckhart Tolle

Yahoo! Even though it's only been a week or so after my second operation to finally release and let go of my embryo, I'd hit August 2013. It was a date that I was getting excited about, because I'd planned a year previous to look at having gastric sleeve surgery. I had to **figure out** how I was going to afford it, knowing what it could give me for my life, my health, and investment in myself. It was something that I'd been looking into for quite a few years. My mum had had a gastric band surgery a few years prior, and I had been a big supporter as her weight was something she'd always struggled with. It was hard as a child to see your mother not being able to do and feel the things that she deserved.

I'd met Dr David Yong 11 months ago, as he was the doctor who did the surgery for my mum. The plan was to get private health insurance to cover my hospital stay, the biggest part of the cost. I'd struggled with my weight over the last decade because of the cancer, the drugs, and not having the physical capability to keep the weight off. The drugs gave me a lot of fluid retention, and there was a lot of physical **side effects** involved in healing from cancer, and taking Glivec. I'd been drug-free for years by this point, and it was time to move faster on losing the weight.

I'd tried many different things; Lite n' Easy, Weight Watchers – you name it, I'd read it, tried it, but hadn't had much success. I had hypothyroidism and that slows down your metabolism. I'd been on Lite n' Easy for a few months and realised I was actually putting weight on. I knew that there was a metabolism problem that I was fighting, so what was I going to do?

Quite a **few years** ago this surgery cost $20-$30,000, but things are different now; there's a lot more science, better results, and there are cost-effective opportunities. I knew that it was going to be an investment of around $3000 at the most, given that I had health insurance. On 20th August I had my first appointment with Dr Yong. I weighed in at 100kgs, the heaviest I'd ever been in my life. I booked a date for the operation for 25th September. I started preparing, and my nutritionist set out rules to get me ready for the operation. For a couple of weeks I was on Optifast to shrink my stomach so that I was in optimal health for the operation.

The day arrived and I was getting settled into the private hospital. I was very excited as I knew it was a decision that was going to change my life forever. All the facts were there; I was definitely going to lose weight as they were going to remove 85% of my stomach. This operation was no walk in the park – it was major abdominal surgery. But for me, the benefits outweighed the risks; I would do anything to have more years to be healthy and vibrant, and to get a spring back in my step. I wanted to keep up with all the things that I wanted to do, and let life begin again. Weight is something that most of us are **dealing with in** some form, trying to lose a few kilograms, trying to find a better way … the amount of money that we put into this industry is just huge.

I was amazed by the fact that eating smaller calorie amounts per day was going to reduce the chance of getting some diseases by **80%**. I always felt in my heart that it should be a human right to be **comfortable** in our bodies so that we can actually just focus on living and not on the stress of being uncomfortable in our own skin. I understood this quite well, because most of my life pre-cancer I was very fit, healthy, and comfortable in my own body, so it was a huge lesson losing that physical ability.

Before I knew I had cancer I would walk and exercise and do everything that I could, but was physically unable to, even to the point where I vomited after aerobics classes because my body wasn't coping with the pressure. I must admit I used to look at people who were overweight and think, 'Oh, you should be doing something more for yourself, why have you let yourself get like this?' Man, did I learn that it's just not that simple. Your health can be taken over by illness and medications and pressures of life. My weight didn't come on suddenly, it was slowly, over a period of time. It was a hard thing to release and let go.

That weight was such a heavy burden. I can remember being invited to a friend's house and wanting to put a nice dress on and feel like I had more energy, and I just didn't. I hid myself for quite a few years, and didn't participate in life because my weight just didn't let me. It limits you. You're **happier to stay** at home and just be by yourself instead of enjoying life and laughing, and having the energy to do that. I knew that having this operation was going to be one of the most important things to help me live a better life. I wasn't sure whether IVF was still going to be something that I would venture down again, but I knew that carrying the weight was not going to help me get pregnant.

I can remember a lot of people being quite surprised about me having this surgery, because they thought it just came out of the blue as I had been concentrating on IVF. The operation went fine, and there were no problems. I spent three days in hospital where I had the most amazing care and was monitored well. I went home and pain was pretty minimal, considering the size of the surgery. It felt like I had a bit of a stitch and had to rest up for a few days, so there was no heavy lifting, pulling, or vacuum cleaning. I started to do a few more things, and as far as eating there wasn't a lot of that going on in the first few weeks; it was purely a liquid diet. It wasn't difficult because you actually just don't feel hungry – your stomach is healing itself, and eating is just the last thing on your mind. Even small amounts of water will make you feel quite full.

It was a little difficult to get used to in the first few weeks, but the schedule was written out. You would slowly introduce more solid foods, protein drinks were very important, and then before I knew it, it was a month later and I was 88kg. By December 2013 I'd already dropped 20kg. That **transformation** was just incredible. I felt so much more vibrant and had more energy, with less pressure to carry myself around. Very quickly I had no clothes that fit me, going from size 16 (and even having 18s in the cupboard) down to 14s, 12s, and eventually 10s. I was even in some size 8s. This was incredible. I was experiencing a whole new me; the weight that this took off mentally was beyond words, let alone the actual weight. I had transformed myself into what I thought was more normal. Some people didn't recognise me at all after the transformation, so I was getting used to shocking people. I started to feel my old self, pre-cancer, the girl I would have been. It felt like I had shed the last decade. I hadn't realised the toll it took on me.

When you've been overweight and then you lose weight, you really notice the difference in how you're treated in society, how people look at you and how people engage, sharing more energy simply because I looked healthier and vibrant. I felt like I went from being invisible to, 'Here I am'. I could not have guessed that the whole energy around me was going to be so, so different – being slimmer resulted in more smiles around me, and customer service in retail just went up! This **attention** affected what I was feeling, things I had not experienced for years. The transformation was intense.

I was feeling like the person I am, a simple human right!

I Am Now

'The past offers you memories. The future offers you **promises**. I am now.'

– Kristie Dean

*I*n 2017, I kept saying to my friends and family that I felt something was going to **happen soon**, that I was going to have some kind of awakening. I believed that in this awakening, something was going to happen to me spiritually, and I was never going to be the same. I was going to look at life differently. I don't really know how I get these feelings, but often in my life I can foresee things, and I often voice it to my family and friends beforehand to give the clarity when what I predict does happen.

It's the beginning of January, and my sister and I planned an amazing 10-day trip to Bali and Lombok. We'd never actually spent time away together because we didn't grow up together, so this was a **huge opportunity** for us to have a special sister bonding time. My sister has three children and they've all grown up, so this allowed us to have time away alone. I think everyone was thinking that this was going to be interesting, because we've both got very strong personalities and the combination of us travelling together could either go horribly wrong, or it was going to blend and be quite easy to be together.

Nicole and I often finished each other's sentences, or we'd find ourselves sitting in a crowd and be thinking the same thing. Even though we didn't grow up together, we have those personal traits because our DNA is just so strong. We are true sisters, as though we'd spent our lives together from the start. From the first day of our trip, everything was like magic. We had the most unbelievable time together, nothing could have gone wrong. We were blessed with great accommodation in Lombok, one of the most **beautiful locations** that either of us had ever been to. We felt very relaxed with each other, had awesome fine food, saw different parts of Lombok, and we'd gone over to the Gili Islands. We planned to do a day trip to the waterfalls because if something spiritual was going to change me, I was going to feel it there. That didn't happen, but the trip was amazing, and I'm so blessed for our **time together**; it was truly awesome, something no money in the world could buy.

After that trip, I made sure that everything was ready for the book I was writing, having all the stages done for the Melbourne book retreat at the end of February. I made sure that all my recordings for each of my chapters were all done so that when I went to the retreat I could relax and learn, and get as much information from all the speakers as I could. However, I just kept saying to my sister and a few others around me that I could feel the last chapter was still in **play,** and that I had to trust my intuition and allow this to happen.

Unfortunately, before flying to Melbourne I started coming down with strong flu symptoms. I managed to push through and get to the retreat, and it was absolutely amazing. We even had media speakers come in. We learnt so much, and this support took me to the next stage. I pressed the button to send all my recordings off to the transcriptionist, everything except the last chapter. In the weeks following that, I would receive my book as a manuscript. It was truly a fabulous retreat, being in the presence of other **powerful** authors. The experience was remarkable, even though the flu was taking me over a little bit. I managed to complete everything that I needed to do and had all the tools for the book to come alive. I felt so blessed to be able to compress all that knowledge into one weekend, and it saved me a lot of time in the process of **writing a book** – you hear of some people starting to write a book and never finishing it just because of the enormity of the project.

I headed back to Perth, and I was still not feeling well. The doctor gave me an antibiotic injection, and I was on different types of antibiotics over the next 3-4 weeks. This put everything on halt for me because I was pretty much bed-bound, because it just wasn't going away. I'd received my manuscript back from the transcriptionist after three weeks and was starting to work through that, but I was struggling because I couldn't focus on anything, and my voice was coming and going.

My girlfriend, Carolyn, who is a herbalist, suggested a few herbs and flower essences to take. I literally spent hundreds of dollars at the chemist, also, taking everything they could suggest to help me feel better. The infection developed in my chest and became bronchitis. What was going on here? I remembered what it was like to be vulnerable again, as I hadn't been sick like this for so many years, and it was a reminder of the many struggles that I'd had in the past. **My voice** was not getting any better, so I thought that there was a little bit more going on than just the flu.

My immune system seemed to be suppressed, and ironically everything was about my throat. I could not seem to push through and get my **voice back** on track. I had noticed that when certain conversations and topics would come up, my voice would just squeak and disappear. I thought this was odd, and that there was something more going on. As a very strong believer that emotional stuff in your life affects the power of your mind and plays a huge part on our health, I believed that not only did I have the flu, but I was struggling with all the emotions of letting go as I had completed most of my recordings for this book. I had to be strong to get through that stage.

I was also working with Jill, my spiritual mother who I first started working with in my teenage years; we'd reunited, and she was helping me over the phone with how I was feeling internally, and sharing some of the spiritual stuff that was coming up for me. Jill believed the struggles stemmed from the suppression of being abused as a young girl. It was all about me finding my voice again, and by writing this book I was standing up very strong and letting go of what I had built inside me by revisiting them.

I had to go through the **last stages** of these again, because even though I'd brought this up to my accuser, there were still a few family members around me who didn't know the full story, and many times over the years I was silenced and never felt comfortable sharing when I was feeling vulnerable at family gatherings. Even though I thought that I'd dealt with it, I hadn't completely cleared everything. I needed my true voice. It was evident to me now that that's what I was going through. The last push of suppressed energy and **emotion in my body** needed to be finally released so that I could be freer and live my true propose, and allow my body the healing it deserved – to be strong enough to stand up and share my story.

In the first week of April I started feeling an extra amount of pressure coming up in my head and body, and the soreness in my throat wasn't getting any better. I knew that it was all spiritually connected to **teaching me** and showing me the way. Again, I set the intentions for this to be released. I spoke for hours with Carolyn, as she knows me well, so she could help me pinpoint and dig deep into some of the fears and thoughts that I had. Later that same day, I had a call with my coach, Mr Jenkins, and that was nothing but awesome. He identified which questions to ask me to locate what was troubling me inside. He has really helped me grow and have a better understanding of myself, and I really appreciate and **respect the value** of having a coach in my life.

After the coaching call, I felt compelled to call Jill to share everything that I was going through. She was guided to perform a distant spiritual healing on me, and I was shown into the future. I felt relief after the spiritual work and, insights received, slept better that night. Jill had mentioned that she was coming into Perth the next day, as she lives down near Mandurah, about an hour south of Perth, and I just felt in my heart that I was meant to see her. I suggested that we spend the afternoon and night together, because I knew that if she could see how my body was that she could help me get through this stage and help me get my voice back. I was ready to finish the last chapter in my book, and have everything come together with clarity so I could share with you all.

Jill and I met up the next day, and we headed out to do some shopping. Afterwards, we went to Trigg Beach for the sunset. While we sat on one of the benches, I was struggling with my voice again, and with the pressure developing in my head; it was painful and uncomfortable. Jill held my hand intermittently as I was coughing and choking, and the healing push began. Suddenly I could **feel more** and more pressure building up in my body, like waves of energy coming from right down in my solar plexus. It's a little bit hard to explain, other than that it felt like a hot air balloon that was stuck inside me, trying to push up through my chest, then neck, and out the top of my head. It felt like I was in some sort of compression chamber.

Clearly something was going on – I could feel my face being pulled and pushed and distorted. We spent about 30 minutes on the bench, and Jill suggested we sit in my car and allow this process to happen in privacy. I couldn't stop this physical release. Lucky I had a box of tissues sitting in the back seat to use. I looked at myself in the rear vision mirror, as I was in the driver's seat and Jill was beside me. I was fascinated by my refection. It didn't look like me; my eyes were different, you could see the pressure around them. The only way I can describe it is if you have ever looked at someone and you see evil in their eyes. I felt a bit like I was possessed with something.

While sitting in the car I was enduring surges of energy coming up through my stomach, my throat, and my eyes. It was hurting; I press my fingers hard on my forehead pressure points to help myself through this strange experience. I felt a bit more relief each time a wave of energy pushed out of me. It was quite exhausting, and we needed to take moments in between each of these experiences. It went on for at least another **half hour**.

Exhausted and overwhelmed, and in a little bit of disbelief, I gathered myself together and verbalized to Jill I'd had enough and wanted to drive home. Jill agreed, but insisted we should finish it off when we got home. She said, 'Kristie, there's a lot more inside you and I want to help you get all this supressed energy out. I believe that you've been pushing it down from the sexual abuse, you've been silenced, and it's ready to come up. You've been working on wanting this feeling outside of you, and the time is now'. We arrived home, and I was thinking, 'Oh, I'm exhausted. That's probably all I can go through today'. But Jill was on a mission, and she didn't give me much of a chance to try to **get out of the situation**. She said, 'Okay, let's do this', so I stood up near my kitchen bench and I faced her. She took my hands, and within seconds I could feel energy just pouring out through me, like a burp of vapour coming up and out my throat.

I found myself being pulled up on my tippy-toes by the strong pressure pushing out through my head and ears. I had no way of stopping this; it was leaving me, something I'd never experienced before. I understood that I could have this suppressed feeling, and that it would be in the form of energy, but feeling it actually go was astonishing. Whenever the air released from my body, I would feel relief.

This continued for undoubtedly a good 40 minutes until I felt it was all out and Jill believed it to be gone. I felt lighter; there was no pressure in my head, and I felt freer, grounded, and very, very relaxed. It was quite remarkable. We gathered ourselves together, and I had a quick shower. As I'm a water baby, this helped me process my thoughts. We headed out to get some dinner. When we were driving home, I noticed I was only driving at 40km, and I said, 'Gosh, Jill, I'm so sorry, I'm just so relaxed'. There was **no hurry** for anything.

I believe this was the spiritual awakening I'd predicted. I would never have guessed it, but it changed me forever. I looked out of my eyes differently from that profound healing experience. Since that day, my throat feels better, I'm feeling better, and there is a peace about me that is new to me. I am sleeping better than I ever have, and I'm just so much more relaxed. I saw a clear vision for the ending of this book. I **have an idea** for a book that will follow this book, and none of that was in my mind before.

It fascinates me that Jill was one of the first people who worked on my body and helped me heal in my early teenage years. We lost contact for 26 years, and I had spent years trying to clear the suppression of that abused childhood. I had been in the Amazon jungle and tried many different natures of healing, but I could never really get that full release that I needed. It was Jill who needed to be the one to guide me through it all, as I needed to feel that **love,** safety, and trust to be able to fully release and let go, and obviously I hadn't been in that space in the past. I feel nothing but completely blessed to have experienced this. To end my book sharing that with you was meant to be.

It's not how I thought I would end the book – it's not what I thought would happen in my life – but it is me, now. I can now say with complete conviction that anyone who has gone through any kind of abuse needs to address it; you need to get it physically out of your body. It's not easy, but it can be done with **unconditional love** and support. I was blessed that day to have unconditional support from my girlfriend, Carolyn, my coach, Jason, and my spiritual healing mum, Jill. Thank you all for **believing me, supporting me, and guiding me.**

I truly believe that my soul was changed.

I am now free.

I am now a strong voice of a sexually, mentally, and physically abused child.

I am now no longer a drug dealer.

I am now a thriving cancer survivor.

I am now a strong, brave, powerful woman.

I am now a published author.

I am now.

So,

Listen, Act, and Thrive.

1993

2017

Jill and Kristie

Your one word?

The **bold** words throughout my book are a **gift to you – my personal, signature tradition** that will always be placed within any books I write.

I enjoy picking up **books randomly**, thinking of a question for guidance, and then flicking open a page and starting to read the sentence or word that catches my eye. This little **ritual** has given me **powerful insights** and often directions to consider or be aware of in my life; a little **tool for fun** and inspiration.

I want to encourage you to join me in this ritual, as I believe and **trust** that everything around us is showing us **signs and guidance** all the time. Life is busy nowadays, so this little ritual stops you and gets you in tune with the moment, and the power of asking the universe for guidance into your next steps on this planet.

There are **no fine rules** to enjoy this ritual – sometimes **flicking open a page** once a day and receiving the one power word will be enough – but maybe you will feel like combining several words to relate to questions on your mind at that moment. Play around with it. It will become stronger the more you use it, so be open to having **fun** and being surprised. Look at it as a **doing mediation.**

If you waited until the end of this book to hear why the bold words appeared, well done to you. **Patience** is a great gift to have … **truly awesomeness**, as I like to say.

I would love to hear about your experience reading my book and using this ritual of power words to **enlighten and guide you**, so please share them with me at www.kristie-dean.com. THANK YOU FOR HEARING MY STORY.

Acknowledgements

I would like to thank all the people in my life whom I call my family.

A **special acknowledgement** to my mother, Vicki, who constantly held the space for me over the years, allowing me to be able to express those shattered moments of my childhood, and being able to help me let go of them. Being my mother hasn't always been easy, and we have gone through all the emotional journeys together. I love you, Mum.

Thank you to my brothers and my one beautiful sister for all your support over the years. A very special thank you to my brother-in-law, Robert Koenig-Luck, for all the professional photos that you've taken for my book, and especially the photo taken for my book cover. It was truly a blessing to have your energy be part of my journey, you have always inspired and supported me. If it wasn't for your brainstorming, the book would not be called *I Am Now*, so thank you, Robert, for being the man you are.

I'd like to acknowledge my soul sister in Switzerland, Rachel Lehar. Thank you for taking all the chapter photos in my book. Having your energy as part of my story is a true blessing.

Also, a special heartfelt thank you to one of my best friends, Carolyn, for your continued support throughout the tough times and the good times. The **synchronicities** and the powerful moments that we continue to share in our life excites me. Thank you very much.

I'd like to acknowledge Natasa Denman, the 48-Hour Author, and Stuart Denman for all your mentoring and your amazing support to make this dream of a book come true. It wouldn't have happened this quickly and professionally without you, and I'm truly, truly blessed to have met you. Friends forever.

Special thank you to everyone at Busybird Publishing – what a fantastic, energetic team.

I'd also like to acknowledge my coach, Jason Jenkins, from Success Coaching. Thank you for your time, your calls, and your support.

Thank you to all my Pilbara community family in Wickham. Thank you for the years that we shared together and the continued support that I get from many of you.

There's hundreds of people behind us in our life that make us who we are today, so I thank every single person for every good and bad experience, because that's who I am today. I'd like to thank you for all the beautiful references and words that you put in my book, because I can truly be blessed with them for the rest of my life. Thank you.

I want to acknowledge anyone who's ever hurt me in my life and made my journey difficult, because that has truly made me who I am today. I'm going to make sure that I take any pain in my life and turn it into power to heal myself and help others, so thank you. I **forgive** you, but I never forget. You may have taken my voice away, but I found it.

Lastly, but very importantly, I thank you all for reading my book and hope that you will keep an open mind to life, and that it will encourage, motivate, and inspire you in your future, because we all have the opportunity to make the most out of this life.

About the Author

Kristie Dean was born in Bunbury, in the south-west of Western Australia, and spent most of her childhood growing up in the small mining town of Wickham, in the north-west.

Kristie is a true survivor, having endured and overcome a mentally, physically, and sexually abusive childhood. Kristie was diagnosed with Chronic Myeloid Leukaemia in her late 20s, and was forced to plead to the Prime Minister to save her life. Kristie appeared in *Sunday Times*, and on *Today Tonight*, *A Current Affair*, and Channel Nine News in 2002, fighting to get access to a life-saving drug.

Kristie, along with a small group of other patients, paved the way to get the drug, Glivec, accessible on the Pharmaceutical Benefits Scheme, making it one of the first smart drugs to be fast-tracked thought the system. It has now not only saved her life, but continues to save many more. Kristie was one of the first in the world to stop taking Glivec, against the advice of her doctors, just trusting her **intuition**. Kristie has remained in remission to this day.

Kristie continues to work on keeping a mentally strong way of life, believing and understanding the power of the mind. She believes you must face your fears head on, releasing and **letting go** of anything that may be holding you back, allowing you to turn any hurt into power. She is very passionate about raising awareness by using and sharing her own life story. She leads the way by opening up about real and very raw topics in her life in the hopes that it will get people talking, sharing, and even healing.

Kristie is now an author, and a contributing author in *The Book of Inspiration for Women by Women*, alongside a collection of other women from around the world, sharing powerful and inspiring messages.

Kristie is director and founder of Infinite Insights Pty Ltd, is a qualified massage therapist, and has certificates in many different modalities. She has helped hundreds of people in **personal development** and healing work over the years, and she will continue to follow her heart and purpose to make a difference; using her life experiences to inspire and motivate others to live the life they deserve.

Kristie is a big-hearted, spiritual woman with a compassionate nature and a huge sense of humour. These drive her passion for making a difference in the lives of others, turning her own survival stories into thriving, powerful teachings.

Kristie now lives in Perth, Western Australia, with her little Maltese dog, Jackals. They love doing Volunteer Pet Therapy work together at aged care facilities. Kristie loves anything that involves the ocean and water. In her spare time you will find her walking, meditating, and even playing her Gasong drum by the beautiful Perth coastline.

About the Author

Connect with Kristie:

    www.kristie-dean.com
    www.towomenbywomen.com
    www.facebook.com/iamnow.com.au
    tokristiedean.neriumaus.com.au

Jackals Dean

Kristie as a Speaker

Kristie Dean is available as a keynote speaker, guest presenter, or trainer/facilitator. Her speaking topics include:

- How to share the power of your own story and write a book.

- How she released and let go of **past trauma**, and turning hurt into power.

- The importance of healing sexual abuse and finding your voice.

- The power your mind has over your body, and her experiences from her cancer journey.

- Experiencing Ayahuasca (plant medicine) in the Amazon jungle.

- Feeling and connecting to your intuition/goal setting, and the power of affirmations.

- Experiencing gastric sleeve surgery, and personal stories of the struggles with being overweight.

- Listening to your intuition, living in the now, and **trusting** your heart's journey.

Coming Soon from Kristie Dean ...

I Was Then
– Exploring Past Lives

These powerful stories of Kristie's past lives explain how ancestral energies and past life experiences created her **pathway** to who she is now.

You have heard her story; you have heard the raw truth. Kristie believes that the patterns of energy that surround her father and her uncle must be explored and dissolved, and never allowed a chance to repeat itself though new generations.

For a warm up to this next book, *I Was Then*, Kristie welcomes you to a glance into the story of her uncle, Paul Harry Dean. This truly needs to be seen to be believed. It is not for the faint-hearted:

www.abc.net.au/4corners/content/2009/s2578036.htm

The journey of your life was planted many souls and lives ago! When we understand the **past**, we realise we have already taken in many lives before this one, and ultimately have a deeper understanding to who we are now. I WAS THEN will take you on a journey through the past, and will guide you on how to start your very own journey of discovery.

www.kristie-dean.com

The book of Inspiration
for women by women

created by
Ruth Cyster-Stuettgen

The Book of Inspirations for Women by Women

Co-authored by Kristie Dean

No. 326 – Admire and Inspire

I believe everything in life happens for a reason, just as you have picked up this book and opened this page. Life will give you signs and lessons that you must be quiet enough to see and hear. So, I say good luck, bad luck – who knows? Observe your life, rather than getting stuck in it. Flow with life and live more in the moment. As they say, the past has gone and the future hasn't happened. I know it's easier said than done, but that's what I think we are truly here to master.

There is a different energy in my life when I accept what is and understand it's not the universe trying to fight me and make things difficult, but guiding me, showing me/helping me/teaching me the important journeys my soul is here to experience. To be! To do! To see and to feel! When you feel your heart beating inside you and you're quiet and still enough, you will feel the answers come to you, **guiding you** to your next journey.

Admire and inspire other women; never come from jealousy. We are here to grow and love each other. Your female relationships will be the most powerful ones you will ever have, so always respect and honor them as that reflects who you truly are. Today, buy two red roses. One is for you, and one is to be given to another woman you **admire.** We are all truly amazing, so shine bright and let life show your destiny …

Always admire and inspire, leaving a little of your sparkle as a footprint wherever you step.

Order your copy at www.towomenbywomen.com

WHERE IS Kristie NOW- updated 2023.

OTHER BOOKS Kristie's Story appears in

- A Journey of the Riches-Making Empowering Choice
- The Book of Inspiration-for women by women

For full details and updates - www.kristie-dean.com

Content Creator /Youtuber

https://www.youtube.com/@KristieDeanADVENTURES

In Kristie's YouTube channel- you will see - Camping equipment - Locations and overviews - Great ideas and Camping hacks & Tricks -Camping setups -Car Camping -Tent Camping, with NOW over 100 videos to inspire all things Camping.

Kristie also shares her creative side with her passion's including Macramé/Pottery/Journal making /Crystals and Rune stones STORIES which bring out Kristie's Spiritual side.

Ladies Camping Australia, Creator and Mentor.

https://www.facebook.com/groups/223899792729455/

This Facebook group has NOW over 23k member and was created by Kristie for Ladies only.

As she has been solo Camping for years NOW and finds more and more other Ladies taking charge of getting outdoors with or without a man around.

Whether you're a single mum or just single with or without a fur pet. Ladies are more than capable to enjoy Camping adventures.

Maybe you have a partner that's not always around when you have the desire to take a Camping trip.

This Group is for ALL Ladies!

So, if you travel with a partner that's welcomed, we can learn from each other's experiences, with Confidence and support we give each other can grow and help Solo Ladies to not be held back from the enjoyment of Camping and healing powers of nature.

This Group welcomes all ladies to share and support likeminded others. Share camping set ups, tips, ideas and photos of places you love to Camp in Australia.

Brand Creator

This design has been a vision by Kristie, for all Ladies Camping Australia.

A design, Ladies can be proud to wear and display on their vehicles, wherever they are from around Australia while in turn Bringing a likeminded community together to support each other.

There are two main base options to Display OR not Display you are in a Ladies Camping Australia community.

The base Design represents ALL Ladies Camping, with a Feather that changes colour's which represents your home State Location.

"WEARING WITH PRIDE IN OUR HEARTS "

Ladies Rising Together

Check out Kristie's online SHOP.

KRISTIE DEAN Shop | Redbubble

Sometimes you need to take time out to reflect, to reconnect, to review. To invest in YOU. To create a consistent space, for a new way of being in the world to shine through.

people. animals. wellness.

Hi there, I'm Carolyn and I am dedicated to helping people & animals with their wellness needs: body, mind and spirit. I love supporting and empowering clients as they (re)connect to their intuition and return to a state of balance and peace that is as individual as they are.

Let's face it: life can be ridiculously busy. Competing demands, the stress of everyday living and time/ circumstance may have lead you towards fatigue or illness. Self-worth issues may have prevented you from stepping forward into the life you know deep down you deserve.

Depending on your unique needs I offer:

- ✓ **Natural medicine consultations:** personalised approach incorporating western herbal medicine, nutrition, hair analysis (food bio-compatibility) and flower essences
- ✓ **Coaching and coaching programs (results focused):** learn how to follow your heart/ joy, honour your intuition, lift your energy, overcome barriers and take action on your dreams
- ✓ **Meditation classes:** learn to meditate *with animals*
- ✓ **Reiki sessions:** for relaxation and healing
- ✓ **Animal Reiki training curriculum:** coming soon!
- ✓ **Anti-aging range:** plant and science based

GIFTS FOR YOU

CLAIM your 20-minute discovery call via Skype (COMPLIMENTARY for all readers: please QUOTE "I AM Now").
Email: Carolyn@pausehq.com.au

GRAB your FREE copy of "Top Five Things Your Animal Friends Want You To Know" when you join the growing Pause community: http://eepurl.com/bNdTTf. (PLUS you'll be kept up to date with the latest blog posts, meditation training dates, special offers & more!)

VISIT the Pause website/blog: www.pausehq.com.au

To your health & happiness xx Carolyn Trethewey

If you would like to find out more about

Kristie's Mentor in the 90s

Sandy MacGregor

Visit

www.calm.com.au

Creative - Accelerated - Learning – Methods

Happiness comes from the journey towards the goal

Learn to forgive, handle fear, anger, anxiety

busybird
publishing
www.busybird.com.au

Want to get published?

We've helped hundreds of authors get their books out into the world!

Whether you're a novellist; a poet; a children's author; a biographer writing about a person, family history, or community; a business person who wants to showcase their expertise to the world; a coach who wants to share their techniques with a greater audience; or a writer of any kind who has a project, Busybird Publishing can help tailor a publishing package to suit your needs!

Let us take care of whatever facets of book production you require – editing, proofing, design, layout, ISBN registration, library deposit, printing, marketing, and so much more.

Call us on **(03) 9434 6365** to have a chat!

Ultimate 48 Hr Author

DO YOU WANT TO BECOME A PUBLISHED AUTHOR?

This book was completed via the Ultimate 48 Hour Author Program. Take the complicated and mysterious journey out of writing a book and work with the experts to help you do it fast, easy and simple.

Ultimate 48 Hour Author runs Preview Events to the Retreat Program Australia Wide where you can experience part of the system for a small investment.

For the Next Date near you simply Contact Them via the Details below.

AFFILIATE CODE: http://bit.ly/2Kristie48HR

BONUS

📞 1300 664 006
✉ book@ultimate48hourauthor.com.au
🌐 www.ultimate48hourauthor.com.au

Notes

aM

Notes

NOW

www.ingramcontent.com/pod-product-compliance
Lightning Source LLC
Chambersburg PA
CBHW021101080526
44587CB00010B/338